WHAT YOU THINK IS WHAT YOU GET

REALIZING YOUR CREATIVE POWER
AND
TRUE POTENTIAL

A No-Philosophy Philosophy

GEORGE LAVENIA

The Earth Foundation
New York

Published by The Earth Foundation
Post Office Box 462
New York, NY   10028

Library of Congress Catalog Card Number: 97-94136

ISBN 0-9658679-0-0

Manufactured in the United States of America

The author of this book does not prescribe the use of any
technique as a form of treatment for physical or medical problems
without the advice of a physician, either directly or indirectly. The
author's intent is only to offer information of a general nature to
assist the reader in reaching emotional and physical well-being.
Should you choose to use any of this information, the author and
publisher assume no responsibility.

Appreciation to Alfred A. Knopf Inc. for permission to reprint
From THE DHAMMAPADA: THE SAYINGS OF THE BUDDHA
by Thomas Byrom, trans. (c) 1976

DEDICATED TO
ALL HUMAN BEINGS
AND THE REALIZATION OF
THEIR REAL SELF AND TRUE NATURE.

We are what we think.
All that we are arises with our thoughts.
With our thoughts we make the world.
Speak or act with an impure mind
And trouble will follow you
As the wheel follows the ox that draws the cart.

We are what we think.
All that we are arises with our thoughts.
With our thoughts we make the world.
Speak or act with a pure mind
And happiness will follow you
As your shadow, unshakable.

How can a troubled mind
Understand the way?

Your worst enemy cannot harm you
As much as your own thoughts, unguarded.

But once mastered,
No one can help you as much,
Not even your father or your mother.

From THE DHAMMAPADA:
THE SAYINGS OF THE BUDDHA
TRANSLATED BY THOMAS BYROM

CONTENTS

CONTENTS

CONTENTS

Contents

PREFACE

Life is a journey on a path to a destination of unknown origin. Each one of us continues on this journey through an evolutionary process of completion and expansion, a series of experiences that can facilitate our personal growth. The purpose of this book is to accelerate that process by focusing your attention inward to reveal the thoughts that are limiting your creative potential and your ability to enjoy a fulfilling life.

This book is written in stages with the intention that you read each chapter in its entirety and in the sequence intended. You could say there are two parts to this work. The first addresses psychological programming and its effects. The second addresses the transformation from the individual idea of self to Universal Consciousness and the experience of one's real Self and true nature.

May your journey be a safe one, free of pain and suffering, and may you find the love, peace, and joy intended as your birthright.

ACKNOWLEDGMENTS

I am eternally grateful to Muktananda Paramahamsa for his devotion to self-realization and perfection and for inspiring me to do the same. My deepest appreciation to Joe Lavenia for his continued support over the years, Adrienne Frimet and Linda Garrett for their editing, and Anya Barkin for her faith in me and her major contributions to this work and to the Earth Foundation.

Ultimately, I acknowledge those who have dedicated their lives to sharing the fundamental truth about our real Self and true nature, and to the miraculous power of love, the sustaining life force within all things.

INTRODUCTION

Let me begin by saying I never felt that I actually wrote this book, but that it wrote itself. After many years in search of a deeper meaning to life and an understanding of my own nature, I was inspired on a path to an inward journey.

As the inspiration grew within me, this book was written, leaving me no choice but to live and experience every aspect of its content. Eventually, this path led to the understanding that we are responsible for creating our own life experiences. With this knowledge also came the obvious realization that being responsible for something also gives a person the power to change it.

The purpose of this book, then, is to empower those who read it with knowledge of their real Self and the experience of their true nature. The empowerment of knowledge doesn't mean adopting new ideas and beliefs to replace the existing ones, but rather operating from a space that is clear and free of the mind's programming.

By holding onto false ideas about ourselves, we limit our growth, resulting in frustration and the constant pursuit to find satisfaction and fulfillment outside ourselves. Forgetful of who we really are and where we come from, we remain lost in fear and uncertainty.

The irony of this situation is that we continue to go about our daily business acting as though we are fine and that life is meant to be this way. It's no wonder we are a lost society living in fear of what tomorrow will bring. We hide from fear, denying it, but remain victims of it just the same. We continue to lie to ourselves and to others in order to mask our true feelings. In fact, we have been living this way for so long that we actually believe our delusional state with all of its self-imposed limitations is the only reality. Fortunately, it is not the only reality, but nothing more than our idea of it.

Our ideas and beliefs distort reality, giving us nothing more than our own point of view. As a result, we spend most of our time seeking pleasure and relief from daily upsets. In this state of dissatisfaction and uncertainty, we unknowingly miss our biggest opportunity to free ourselves. We remain unaware that those very experiences we work so hard to avoid provide the biggest opportunity to free us.

Upon realizing our heritage and reestablishing our relationship with the Creative Source, the limitations we have identified with no longer have an effect on our lives. Out of this freedom, we realize our true potential and the opportunity that exists for all humanity. The realization that this opportunity lies within our grasp is uplifting. This understanding rejuvenates our spirit, enhancing our ability to communicate and experience the innate love we have for one another.

~

WHAT IS LIFE'S WORTH
IF NOT TO LEARN FROM EACH EXPERIENCE?

~

CHAPTER 1

GENERATION AFFECTING GENERATION

*"There was a child went forth every day,
And the first object he look'd upon,
that object he became."*

Walt Whitman

Born into this world uncertain of our origin, we have no choice but to learn from the examples set by others. This process of receiving secondhand knowledge doesn't present a problem unless the people we come in contact with are lost and out of touch with who they really are. That being the case, we would pick up qualities that are unlike our real Selves and develop beliefs contrary to our true nature.

The following is a story I have taken the liberty of embellishing in order to shed light on the above.

A very long time ago, a group of fearless lions roamed the earth. Since they were kings of all the land, they were free to do whatever they pleased and to go wherever they wanted. However, they wanted so much out of life that they soon lost control. They began fighting over the very things they themselves had power over: the land, the food, and all that was theirs to share.

In all of the excitement, the lions soon forgot they were kings who reigned over everything in the land, including the very things they were fighting over. Having forgotten their heritage, the lions began to act contrary to their true nature. They spent most of their time frantically storing food so they could feel secure. Imagine! The kings of a kingdom believing they had to worry about their security and well-being!

This worrisome way of life soon became an unwanted responsibility. Feeling the pressure of the situation they had created for themselves, they began to look for more in order to relieve the frustration. Their desire for food and sex became insatiable, and the need for self-gratification grew to enormous proportions. Soon they were no longer acting like lions at all but rather like helpless monkeys living in fear of one another, quarreling over their differences in a desperate attempt to survive.

As time went on, the lions had cubs of their own. These impressionable cubs naturally depended on their parents to guide them. Unfortunately, what the cubs found were lions swinging from trees like frantic monkeys. The parents were in such a frenzy they weren't capable of giving their own children the love they needed to grow up with a sense of well-being. This lack of love had an adverse effect on the cubs, who grew up believing they, too, were weak, helpless monkeys. After all, everyone around them acted this way, so why should they believe otherwise?

According to tradition, the parents decided the time had come to teach the cubs about their Creator and the power inherent within each of them. The cubs, having lost respect for their parents, didn't take what they had to say seriously. Consequently, the cubs did not believe they were kings and descendants of the Almighty. Now grown up and carrying this burden with them, they passed this feeling of helplessness onto their own cubs who also grew up affected by the same beliefs.

So now, instead of lions roaring and demonstrating their inherent power, we have lions howling and swinging from the trees like monkeys, a condition destined to continue until they stop and ask the question, "Who am I?" and begin the journey inward to find the answer.

~

DON'T
BELIEVE
THAT WHAT YOU SEE
IS THE WAY IT WAS MEANT TO BE,
BECAUSE IF YOU DO, LIFE
WILL BE THAT
WAY FOR
YOU.

~

Chapter 2

Your Relationship with Your Parents and Its Effect on Your Life

*"The imitativeness of our early years
makes us acquire the passions of our parents,
even when these passions poison our lives."*

Stendhal

When you arrived on this planet, the first impressions you received influenced the makeup of your personality. In most cases those impressions came from experiences with your parents. In those early years, you distinguished between pleasurable and painful experiences. Wanting nothing to do with painful situations, you avoided them by going into a state of partial unconsciousness. What this means is the mind's auto response mechanism took over to protect you. It's similar to losing consciousness when you're in a serious accident.

By trying to avoid these feelings, you buried those memories deep within your subconscious. Burdened by those memories, you remain at their effect, causing you to *act out* your anger on others, and when the outburst is over, you take little or no responsibility for your ill behavior. In fact, you act as though you have the right to get upset at others when they don't conform to your way of thinking. What's even worse, this behavior is so ingrained in you it seems as though you can't stop yourself. Blinded by emotions and running on your reactive mind, you become nothing more than an extension of your parents, acting the same way toward others as your parents acted towards you.

SO WHO'S TO BLAME

As a child you were the one who decided to get upset. No one forced you to look at things the way you did. Your parents didn't make you get upset; getting angry was your choice. Of course your parents are responsible for their actions; however, this is not about your parents. This is about getting you to take responsibility for your negative feelings in order to free yourself from their effect.

The situations that brought about your feelings of anger and resentment toward your parents are real. No one is denying that. Those things really happened, and because your feelings are valid and not merely a figment of your imagination, you believe you are justified in holding onto them. Thinking this way makes it impossible for you to let go of the negative feelings you harbor for your parents. Unless you let go of those feelings, you will continue to be affected by them, causing you to unleash your anger indiscriminately onto others.

To free yourself of these feelings, you can begin by realizing why you ended up with the parents that you did. Simply stated, you were born into this world in the exact place and circumstance that reflects your level of consciousness, meaning your temperament matched perfectly with that of your parents. In other words, the experiences you and your parents shared together were the experiences necessary to further your growth as well as theirs. That's why you and your parents came together. In fact, your relationship with your parents is not only the perfect one for you, it's the only one. If you are willing to accept this relationship and understand it is no accident, you will find reconciliation.

LETTING IT GO

It's not enough to know you are responsible for the parents you have. You must take the next step and find the compassion necessary to forgive them for what you believe they did to you. Before judging your parents, consider this: your parents had parents too. As a result, your grandparents affected your parents, causing your parents to react the way they did toward you. One can only assume the reason you didn't consider this before passing judgment on your parents is that your anger goes so deep, you were blinded by it. Perhaps you are so incensed with their actions that you want to get even with them regardless of the circumstances. The fact is you are a reflection of your parents' consciousness, just

10

YOUR RELATIONSHIP WITH YOUR PARENTS AND ITS EFFECT ON YOUR LIFE

as they are a reflection of yours. Ultimately, there is no difference between you and your parents. You could say: you and your parents are one and the same.

As you can see, no one is really to blame. But we blame our parents just the same. I'm not suggesting that people are not responsible for their actions. Rather, no one is to blame because all of us are running on programmed responses.

If anything, you should ask yourself why you haven't taken responsibility for your feelings and the actions associated with them. You can begin taking responsibility for your feelings right now by breaking the chain that links you to this programming. Simply *stop reacting toward others with anger and hostility*. You can stop this addictive behavior. It can be done but you have to start somewhere, and a good place for you to start is by forgiving your parents. That means really forgiving them, not merely scratching the surface and paying lip service to the idea, but really getting deep inside the place where you harbor these feelings. Isn't it time to let go of these negative feelings once and for all?

It might help you to remember that whatever people do, they do from their level of consciousness. That means whatever oppressive things your parents did, they really didn't know any better or they wouldn't have done them. Judging others and persecuting them

11

for their actions shows a lack of understanding and compassion. Remember, no matter what your parents did, they did the best they could.

Your parents are not to blame. Accepting this and taking responsibility for your actions will help you to find the compassion necessary to forgive them which is the key to freeing you from the anger, resentment, and guilt you carry.

~

LOVE IS THE WAY,
TRUTH IS THE ANSWER,
SO WHY HOLD ONTO THOUGHTS
THAT GROW LIKE A CANCER?

~

CHAPTER 3

THE REASONS BEHIND OUR LOVE

*"You cannot endure yourselves
and do not love yourselves sufficiently;
so you seek to entice your neighbor to love you
and gild yourselves with his error."*

Friedrich Nietzsche

When we fall in love with a special person, often it's that we've found someone who fulfills our needs. As long as the ego is getting what it wants, we feel wonderful. Unfortunately, this euphoria is only temporary because once the ego is satisfied, the honeymoon is over.

The problem is that if we base love on external things, we will try to get the love we need from others. Searching outside ourselves for love causes us to ponder questions such as, "Am I the one he loves the most?" or "How much does she love me?" Because of insecurity we're always looking for the answers to questions like these. The truth is when you say, "I love you" to someone special, what you're really saying is, "I need you, so tell me you need me too."

If your love comes with wants and needs, it's like an appendage you carry with you wherever you go.

Looking for love while holding onto these desires will never allow you to find it. Unfortunately, the search to fill the void inside will go on in vain until you ask the right question, and the reason you don't ask the right question is that you're unwilling to hear the answer.

One might think, after having such a difficult time trying to find love, you would question your motives. But rather than inquiring, you continue looking for love in all the wrong places. Don't misunderstand; I don't mean simply finding someone and spending time with that person. I'm talking about being in relationships that are fulfilling and nurture growth. And that doesn't mean relationships with people you depend on for your happiness. You see it's impossible to experience real love if you have ulterior motives for loving. To experience love for others, you must love them simply because you love them, and that means loving them unconditionally.

~

IF YOUR CHOICE TO BE IN A RELATIONSHIP
IS BASED ON YOUR NEEDS, YOU
CANNOT EXPECT THAT
RELATIONSHIP TO BE FULFILLING.
WHAT YOU CAN EXPECT IS
DISAPPOINTMENT,
DISSATISFACTION,
AND DESPAIR.

~

LIVING YOUR OWN LIE

We avoid the truth about love because we want to believe it's possible to feel love for some and hate for others. We rationalize this belief and avoid honest inquiry into it because revealing the lie we're living would disrupt our lives. We want the truth to be *our way* of thinking because if it isn't, our belief system would be shattered and we would have to take a serious look at ourselves and the way we live our lives.

The next time you're frustrated and angry with someone, take a look at yourself. If you're honest, you will acknowledge the beast within you. Why do you think it's possible to be angry and harbor a beast inside of you, and at the same time be capable of expressing

18

love from the heart? Truly, it's not possible. The beast within must go.

Since all things come from one source, how can we believe it is possible to love one part of this creation and not another? The conflict of loving one person and hating another will never allow us to experience real love and its unlimited power. Certainly we can disagree with others, but fundamentally we have love in our hearts for everyone. This is a hard fact that we're unwilling to face because it invalidates our beliefs, revealing the lie we're living.

The answer to completing this endless search for love is simple. Stop looking for love outside of yourself. This is the most logical conclusion, since trying to get satisfaction externally doesn't work. Considering that looking for love outside of yourself hasn't worked for you or anyone else, what you're looking for must be within you. So learn to look within, and you will find what you have been seeking.

~

IF
YOUR LOVE
IS BASED ON YOUR
OWN CONCEPT—A CONCEPT THAT
YOU HAVE ADOPTED IN ORDER TO FULFILL
YOUR WANTS, NEEDS, AND DESIRES—
YOU'LL NEVER KNOW
REAL LOVE OR ITS
UNLIMITED
POWER.

~

Chapter 4

WANTS AND NEEDS
HOW THEY RUN YOUR LIFE

*"The animal needing something
knows how much it needs,
the man does not."*

Democritus of Abdera

If you observe yourself closely, you will see how your wants and needs influence every aspect of your life. For example, if you want a promotion at work, you most likely begin to act out others' expectations. Or perhaps you want to be part of a particular social set, so to be accepted, you begin to act like the people who are part of that group. If you're looking for a mate, you might change your hairstyle, buy a new wardrobe, or do any number of things to attract the person you want.

Your choice of a gift for someone is another example. What you choose and why you choose it will most likely have something to do with fulfilling your wants and needs. You may think you are doing something for another person, but has it ever occurred to you that what you're actually doing might be for yourself, for example, giving a gift, paying a compliment, or offering to help someone in order to relieve your guilt, or to feel loved? One thing is certain; if you are not free of wants, needs, and desires, most of what you do in life is self-serving, even when you think it's for your loved ones.

~

WE RARELY EXPRESS WHO WE REALLY ARE.
INSTEAD, WE PORTRAY WHAT WE NEED TO BE
TO GET WHAT WE WANT.

~

ATTRACTING YOUR COUNTERPART

If you have a need to be treated a certain way, you will attract a personality type that will fulfill those needs. For example, if you're insecure, you may attract someone who is forceful and domineering. Perhaps you have guilt feelings and a subconscious need to be punished, so you choose someone who treats you poorly and criticizes you.

Whether we realize it or not, we pick people who treat us the way they do because we have a need to be treated that way. These kinds of needs exist on a subconscious level, so we are unaware of them, but they influence our lives just the same.

~

YOUR NEEDS RUN YOUR LIFE.
LOOK CLOSELY AT YOUR LIFE EXPERIENCES,
AND YOU WILL SEE WHAT YOUR NEEDS ARE.

~

UNDER THE INFLUENCE

One of the drawbacks of being motivated by needs is that you limit your awareness to what can satisfy those needs. In other words, you only see what you're looking for, which contributes to your unconscious state. Unaware of your surroundings, you lose your sense of being an integral part of the whole. This loss reinforces the illusion of individuality and separateness. Making personal needs a priority in life, you lose touch with your real Self and true nature, and become nothing more than a robot running on its programming. Functioning with your needs as your priority, you are driven by your desire to get what you want.

The irony is, although you're the one responsible for creating the situation you find yourself in, you then ask, "Where has all the love gone and why isn't there peace and harmony on earth?" You ask, "Where is God and why doesn't He do something?" Now let's ask the real question to the right person. WHAT ABOUT YOU?

Why don't you do something? Why don't you take responsibility for creating the world you live in? What are you waiting for, someone else to blame?

~

WHAT YOU
FEEL YOU NEED
IS WHAT YOU WANT,
AND WHAT YOU WANT,
WHETHER YOU REALIZE IT OR NOT,
IS WHAT YOU'VE GOT.

IN ORDER TO MOVE ON,
ACCEPT IT.

~

CHAPTER 5

SEX AND THE SEARCH FOR LOVE

"Love is not measured
by how many times you touch each other
but by how many times you reach each other."

Cathy Morancy

There are many hidden feelings linked to sexual desires, all of which come from a need for love. In an attempt to quench this thirst, we involve ourselves in romance after romance. The need to fill this void within keeps us in hot pursuit of the sexual experience. Unfortunately, trying to find love through sexual gratification goes on in vain. We do nothing more than satisfy this desire for short periods of time, only to find it burning deep within us once again. This is the reason we put so much emphasis on sex and why many of us can't control our sexual desire.

Acceptance is a big part of the sexual experience. We want to satisfy our partner, not so much because we love him or her but because we want that person to want us. We hope if our partner likes the way we make them feel, we will be wanted. This sense of being wanted temporarily fills our emptiness with the false belief that we are loved. Conversely, when we are on the receiving end, we deceive ourselves into thinking we are loved, when in truth our partner is merely fulfilling his or her desire, which in turn satisfies our own.

At times, the desire to fulfill this need for love can be so overwhelming that the tension from fear of rejection renders some people physically dysfunctional. In all of its forms, the attempt to find love by external means leads us on a long and empty road to nowhere.

CAUGHT IN THE FIRE

If you are one of those people whose life revolves around sex, it will be revealing for you to observe your thoughts throughout the day, especially when you're with someone you are physically attracted to. This type of observation will reveal the kinds of sexual thoughts you're having that stimulate and program your mind into always wanting more.

Be aware of how you take notice of others or how you might fantasize about being in a relationship with them. With all of this internal dialogue, you are continually programming your mind to have physical desires that cause you to feel as though you want and need something more. Now, influenced by those thoughts, you are stimulated by what you see, and what you see is influenced by the images you've programmed into your mind. Operating in this manner is similar to a dog chasing its own tail. This kind of thinking limits your consciousness, causing you to look for someone outside yourself to fulfill the need for love. And since this need for love is misconstrued to be a physical need, anyone physically attractive to you will do.

Unfortunately, once the right person comes along and the physical attraction wanes, so does the possibility of getting the love you need. So the relationship becomes boring and less fulfilling. At this point in the relationship, you blame the other person and decide he or she is not the right one. Then you start looking for someone else, or you stay in the relationship resenting the other person.

FREEDOM FROM THE DESIRE

To free yourself from sexual obsession, stay awake. Expose your fantasies by paying close attention to every thought and feeling. From now on, when you participate in a sexual act, stay alert. Allow yourself to experience it exactly as it is without your added interpretation. Witness the act. Keep your eyes open and look at your partner rather than turning the lights off or closing your eyes and fantasizing. Be there, in the moment, and accept whatever happens without judging it.

When you stay awake and consciously witness the physical act, the mind-thoughts associated with the physical desire get played out. The same thoughts that once had the power to seduce you no longer have any power over you. Of course, if you go into a semi-conscious state during the act, or you fantasize about it later, you will end up with the original mind-thought that seduced you as well as a new thought impression that will increase your sexual desire still further.

Staying aware of your thoughts and observing your actions gives you the power to control your desires. That way, you can be free to tune into and experience reality rather than your idea of it. Remember: stay awake, be aware of your thoughts, and put all of your attention on what is actually happening and not your interpretation of it. At the same time, don't deceive yourself about your feelings or resist your physical desires. Simply experience and complete your desires without continuing to create more of the same. Most of all don't forget to enjoy yourself.

~

IF YOU CONTINUE TO PURSUE YOUR SEXUAL
DESIRE WITHOUT INQUIRING
INTO ITS SOURCE, YOUR
SEXUAL DESIRE WILL
CONTINUE TO
PURSUE
YOU.

~

CHAPTER 6

THE DIFFERENCE BETWEEN WORK AND PLAY

*"When work is a pleasure,
life is a joy!
When work is duty,
life is slavery."*

Maxim Gorky

The difference between work and play is nothing more than your preconceived idea about the activity. It may sound crazy, but it's true. Whether you like or dislike doing something has nothing to do with your activities because your point of view dictates your experience of those activities.

It's no secret that most people dislike going to work; however, you could be doing something very strenuous or even dangerous and experience it as fun. For example, some people will try to hit a small ball over a net with a racket, lose the game, and still say it was fun, while others will carry a bag of clubs on their back for hours in hope of using them to hit a tiny ball into a small hole. Or you may be one of those people who derive pleasure from picking up a sixteen-pound ball with three fingers and rolling it down an alley in order to knock down some wooden pins. On the other hand, you might enjoy risking your life by hanging off sheer cliffs in an attempt to climb to the top of a mountain.

The interesting thing about these examples is that, when you're finished with activities like these, you say you had a great time and can't wait to do it again. But when it comes to your job, where less may be required, you call that *work* and have a negative feeling about it.

Although you may find these examples humorous, I can assure you they are not. If anything, finding humor in this behavior shows just how far you have strayed from the truth. That you don't take the time to look at what you do and why you do it is your misfortune. Unknowingly setting yourself up for dissatisfaction when you hold the key to your fulfillment is a great travesty, and only you can correct what you have done.

THE TRUTH REVEALED

The way you feel about doing something is directly related to the way you think. By choice, you are the one who determines the amount of enjoyment you get out of your pursuits. In fact, you can get satisfaction from everything you do by giving yourself *totally* to all of your endeavors. However, the only way you can experience that kind of freedom is when you no longer associate survival with what you're doing. That way, you're not attached to the outcome, which means *you*

35

have nothing to lose. Now here's the whole thing in a nutshell. If you have nothing to lose, there's no fear, and if you have no fear, you're free—free from any idea associated with what you do.

∽

ONCE YOU GIVE UP YOUR CONCERN
ABOUT WHAT YOU'RE DOING,
YOU CAN BE FREE OF FEAR,
AND THAT'S THE ONLY
DIFFERENCE BETWEEN
WORK AND PLAY.

∽

By letting go of your concerns, you are free of your mind's influence. Then and only then can you get as much enjoyment out of work as you do from play. Then you can come *from* enjoyment rather than trying to find it. It's that simple!

As you can see, the way you experience something is totally up to you. To use this knowledge is your birthright—your right to create the experience of joy in your life. Since you are reading this right now, one can only assume your time has come to accept what's yours—the joy and satisfaction that come out of doing whatever you do. Congratulations!

~

THERE IS NO DIFFERENCE
BETWEEN WORK AND PLAY OTHER
THAN HOW YOU CHOOSE TO LOOK AT IT.

~

CHAPTER 7

FREEING YOURSELF FROM UPSETS

*"There is nothing either good or bad
but thinking makes it so."*

William Shakespeare

We spend most of our lives trying to control, manipulate, change, or totally avoid what arises in life. We feel as though life is something we have to contend with on a daily basis. This struggle is like being on a roller coaster with endless ups and downs. However, life itself is constant change. If you forget that, you will suffer over the very changes themselves. By holding onto your idea of how things should be, you become the cause of your own suffering. All that is required to free yourself from life's upsets is to stop judging the experiences that come up for you.

By constantly looking at things from your point of view, you invariably end up in conflict. The reason for this is that what occurs in life—*what is*—is never the same as the way you see it. In fact, it never will be the same as long as you continue to look at things from one point of view or another. The real problem is not *what* is occurring in your life but rather your unwill-ingness to accept things the way they are, coupled with your obsession with wanting everything your way. If you take a look at the innumerable possibilities of what can occur in life, you must admit it's foolish to get upset when things don't go the way you'd like. More importantly, if you insist on holding onto the way you want things to be, *a majority of the experiences in your life will be upsets.* Operating that way doesn't make any sense. At best, it's a rough way to go through life.

∽

WITH EVERY PROBLEM A SOLUTION IS BORN.

SO DON'T DWELL ON THE PROBLEM,

LOOK FOR THE SOLUTION.

∽

THE BURDEN OF RESPONSIBILITY

Responsibilities can be upsetting. It doesn't necessar-ily matter whether it's a responsibility that was cast upon you or one that you happily chose. A good example is a promotion at work that you have been anxiously await-ing. In time this long-awaited opportunity and the work associated with it become burdensome—something you feel you have to do and must contend with.

You see even when we want something and get it,

it usually ends up as something we would rather not have to deal with. This example shows you that, if you continue to believe you have the right to have things your way and not the way they are, you will always be disappointed.

~

YOU'LL BE A LOSER IN THE GAME OF LIFE
IF YOU TRY TO CHANGE LIFE
SO IT WORKS YOUR WAY.
TO WIN, ACCEPT IT
THE WAY IT IS.

~

CHANGE

Become aware of how many things you do with a negative attitude. Catch yourself when you are triggered emotionally. By doing so you stop wasting energy. This additional energy can be used as a catalyst in freeing yourself even further. Oddly enough, your biggest opportunity to liberate yourself from upsets comes when you're upset.

It's reassuring to know that your choices determine the number of upsets you will encounter in your life. Having this knowledge, you'll realize how foolish it is not to accept everything that comes up in your life, since whatever it is, has already taken place. This does-n't mean that, if a situation is not working out satisfac-torily, you do nothing about it. Quite the contrary. If something can be done to improve a situation, simply do it without complaining.

~

IF
YOU ACCEPTED
THE THINGS IN LIFE
THAT YOU DISLIKED DOING,
EVERYTHING YOU DID WOULD
BE THE SAME AS DOING EVERYTHING ELSE.
AND IF EVERYTHING YOU DID WAS THE SAME
AS DOING EVERYTHING ELSE,
EVERYTHING WOULD BE
OKAY.

SO,
EVERYTHING IS OKAY.
GET IT?

~

NO ESCAPE

As long as you're on this planet, there will always be something for you to do, and as long as you think of doing things in terms of "having" to do them, you'll be the loser in life. Moreover, have you ever tried doing the things you like for an extended period of time? In many cases what you're doing gets boring. So, you're off again looking for something better to do.

The odds will always be against you if you continue to look for things to relieve yourself from your so-called problems. At best, you can be happy sometimes and have many problems and upsets most of the time.

~

IF
YOU
STOPPED
RESISTING THE
SITUATIONS THAT UPSET YOU,
YOU WOULD BE FREE FROM THEIR EFFECT,
SINCE IT'S YOUR RESISTANCE TO
SITUATIONS THAT CAUSES
YOU TO GET UPSET
OVER THEM.

YOU SEE,
LIFE IS PERFECT THE WAY IT IS.
AND ALL YOU HAVE TO
DO TO ENJOY IT
IS ACCEPT IT
THAT
WAY.

~

CHAPTER 8

MEDITATION

"If you regulate your body
and unify your attention,
the harmony of heaven will come upon you.
If you integrate your awareness,
and unify your thoughts,
spirit will make its abode with you."

Chuang - Tzu

The primary purpose of meditation is to experience a space deep within you that is clear and free of thought. By focusing your attention on your inner being, you can regain your natural ability to function unobstructed by limiting mind-thoughts. What meditation is not about is trying to stop your mind-thoughts. Trying to stop the mind's incessant rambling is in vain, and attempts to erase the mind's programming are futile. The die has been cast and the program written. However, by focusing on the space between thoughts and centering your attention there, you can reside in a state of perpetual calm. You can experience a realm beyond all expectation, the source of unlimited potential and infinite possibilities.

To begin, find a place where you can sit quietly in a dark room without being disturbed. If you're using a chair, do not use the backrest unless you find it absolutely necessary. The seat of the chair should be firm, and you should position yourself on the front portion of it so you do not sink down into it. If you're sitting on the floor with your legs crossed, you may find it helpful to elevate your buttocks. Elevating your buttocks off the floor will take the pressure off your legs.

Sitting upright, straighten and elongate your spine by lifting the crown of your head up toward the ceiling. Align your head with your spine; your head should not be tilted forward or backward. Now locate your body's center by positioning your body so that you can sit upright with your back balanced effortlessly. Picture a spinning top with its focal point directly at its center, or a yardstick aligned from the bottom of your spine to the top of your head. You should be able to sit effortlessly without feeling as though you have to continually adjust your position. Rest your hands on your knees with your palms facing up or down. The intention is to remain in a comfortable position with little or no movement. Once comfortable with your posture, be still. If any part of your body becomes stiff or uncomfortable, stretch or shift your position, taking care not to disrupt your concentration any more than necessary.

Now close your eyes and focus your attention inward. Breathing through your nose and with your mouth closed, begin by exhaling. The reason for exhaling first is to maximize the capacity of your air intake. Now, taking a long slow breath in, expand the lower portion of your abdomen like a balloon. Continue to inhale, contracting the lower portion of your abdomen slightly as you bring the air upward, expanding and filling the upper portion of your chest. Imagine the air going up to the top of your head. Now reverse the process. Begin exhaling slowly from your upper chest and then from your abdomen, contracting it slightly in order to maximize your next inhalation.

Take full deep breaths, but do not strain yourself or force the air in either direction. The movement should be smooth and flowing. As you inhale and exhale, listen to the sound of each breath you take. A simple way to find the sound of your breath is to cover your ears with your hands and listen for the echo sound of your breath where your nasal passages meet the back of your throat. Once you find the sound of your breath place your hands back down on your knees. Stay focused on the sound of your breath, letting it draw you deeper and deeper inward. As you become more proficient at this process, begin to increase the volume of air, remembering not to strain or force yourself.

Continue to focus your attention inward and become aware of your thoughts. Begin to watch them but do not engage them; that is, remain detached and don't follow your thoughts or get involved in the content of the dialogue. In other words, don't daydream or talk to yourself. If you find yourself caught up in your mind-thoughts, simply let them go. Separate yourself from them by witnessing your thoughts from a distance. Don't allow yourself to become attached to the details of the thoughts. Remind yourself that this is the time you have decided to use to be free of thought. You will have plenty of time to address the importance of these thoughts once you have finished, and that time comes when you decide, not when your mind lures you into thinking.

The next step is simple. Stop listening to your breath and begin breathing naturally. Don't be concerned about your breathing. As you continue, your breathing may slow down to short breaths, and it may even stop for a brief period. Again, don't be concerned with your breath. Let yourself go deeper and deeper into the void within. If thoughts come up, simply let them go without getting frustrated. Pay no attention to them. Just let go of them as if they were clouds floating away, continuing to center your attention on the open space between the thoughts. Now focus your consciousness on your consciousness. That's right! Focus your awareness on your awareness and develop a firm sense of this state. Allow yourself to be enveloped in this awareness. Let it permeate every part of your being. This conscious awareness is the very essence, the Source and the ground of your being.

If during this process different emotions come up for you, don't avoid or suppress them. Remain open and willing to experience them. This is not unusual, and you shouldn't be concerned or let yourself become distracted. If anything, you should be pleased to know you are in touch with emotions that have been buried deep within your subconscious. More importantly, this is an accelerated approach to completing those feelings, freeing you from their effect.

By clearing your mind and remaining centered in this space for extended periods of time, you can cut through the thoughts linked to past experiences that have a negative impact on your life. These controlling thoughts are directly related to your *karma*, an eastern philosophical term meaning action, which in this case pertains to a person's actions and the effect they have on one's life.

If you intend to participate in this process, then do so with vigor and determination. Be relentless in your pursuit and make it a life-long commitment. Every morning, in the afternoon whenever possible, and in the evening before going to sleep, sit quietly and focus inward for a minimum of twenty minutes. According to the level of clarity and focus you are achieving, you may find it beneficial to increase this time to as much as three hours a day. Don't panic; the extended time is a goal for the future, not something you're expected to achieve immediately or, for that matter, something that is necessary to reap the benefits of meditation.

Don't make the mistake of forgetting about this

process because you think it's not the right time or place. In other words, you don't have to be sitting in a quiet room. Regardless of the situation, continue to focus your attention inward, listening to your breath and bringing yourself back to the present every time you catch yourself daydreaming. The more you apply yourself, the more you will benefit.

THE CALL TO ARMS

I assume that since you are still reading, you have decided to go ahead with this process. If so, I acknowledge you for your bravery and for your willingness to take your first step as a peaceful warrior. Don't be surprised if at first it seems as though you are in a battle. In fact, you are in a battle fighting the same war you've always been fighting. The only difference now is that you have found your adversary, and it's you; that is, it's something you have identified with that's in conflict with you, and it's your ego.

This conflict is all about control, which tells you something about your adversary. It's afraid to lose control, and fear in any form is always based on survival. Therein lies the information you need to defeat your adversary. The fact that your ego lives in fear and needs to be in control lets you know you shouldn't try to engage it head-on because fighting it on its terms is a losing battle. If you do, you will only give your ego strength. Remember that your ego thrives on conflict.

In order to free yourself from your ego's grasp, you must disengage when it tries to provoke you. Don't let your ego lure you into battle. Take the air from under its wings, defuse it, and take away its power. The way to accomplish this is by not allowing yourself to get frustrated or angry. For example, don't be impatient with others for their mistakes or criticize them for their errors. Treat everyone with respect. Remember that everyone, including yourself, is under the same influence of the beast within (ego), so don't blame or judge others for their actions. If anything, you should have compassion and understanding, knowing that when a person is overcome by his or her ego, that person is creating negative karma for himself or herself.

Most of all, never forget that your adversary—*your ego—is nothing more than a figment of your imagination,* which means you are the only one who has influence over your ego. It also means that you can feed your ego or you can starve it to death. Once again, the choice is yours.

~

A MIND
ALLOWED TO WANDER
IS LIKE A WILD ANIMAL ON THE PROWL.
LEFT UNATTENDED, IT
WILL EAT YOU
ALIVE.

~

CHAPTER 9

POSSESSED BY YOUR POSSESSIONS

*"Attachment is the great fabricator of illusions;
reality can be attained only by someone
who is detached."*

Simone Weil

Are you so attached to your possessions that you become upset when they get slightly damaged? Are you so obsessed with the things that are special to you that you can't really enjoy them? When separated from your possessions, do you worry about them and become concerned over their safety? Do you ask friends to keep an eye on things when you're away so that you can relax and not worry about the things you own? Do you feel as though you haven't anything to wear even though you have a closet full of clothes? When you go shopping, do you buy things you really need, or are you often compelled to buy things you see and feel you must have?

I'm sure you would agree that we need material things to function in this world, but is it really necessary to become so attached that we become possessed by what we own? Of course, you could try to achieve non-attachment by getting rid of everything you own, but you will still have the same problem because divesting yourself of your belongings won't rid you of your possessive tendencies.

There is a way to enjoy what you have without being attached and that's by letting go of your belief that the things you own are necessary for your happiness, your prestige, or your security. As long as you associate your happiness with your possessions, you can never be happy with them. You will always have the need to acquire new things that are better, or at best, you'll feel the need to keep a watchful eye on what you have.

As you can see, this is a game you can't win, and once you realize that, you open yourself to the possibility that life can work with what you have and that getting more doesn't make life any better.

~

IF MORE WERE BETTER,
EVERY TIME YOU GOT MORE
YOU WOULD BE SATISFIED.

WELL, ARE YOU?

~

CHAPTER 10

THE GAMES PEOPLE PLAY

"All the world's a stage,
And all the men and women are merely players . . ."

William Shakespeare

If you observe closely, you will see how most people use various acts to suit the situation they find themselves in. For instance, if you're feeling insecure while having a conversation, you may begin to act very knowledgeable about the topic in hope of having people believe you know what you're talking about. Another ploy is to act weak and helpless so others will take pity on you. Then we have the "Yes, I agree" act. That's the one where you agree with what someone else says because you don't want to be put on the spot for fear of looking foolish. You simply assume a safe position in the conversation.

Perhaps one of your acts is to be complacent and noncommittal when it comes to making a decision. If you're really put on the spot, you may act confused and incapable so others will take pity on you and make decisions for you. Of course, if the act doesn't work and you get stuck having to do something you don't want to do, you can always do a poor job. This act ensures that no one will ever ask you to do that job again.

As if all this were not enough, we also have beliefs about the appropriate behavior based on our parents' admonishments. For example, as children we were programmed by hearing things such as "Why don't you stop that nonsense and *act* like a grown up?" or "Why can't you *act* more like your brother? He's such a *good* boy." In addition to these constant reminders, we saw the adults around us acting differently from the way they really felt, leading us to believe that hiding our true feelings was the right thing to do.

It would seem as though we have our lives all worked out—an act for every occasion, a drug to suit our every need, and a therapist to help us deal with our problems. But even with all of these remedies, can you honestly say that your life is working? Are you relaxed with everyone you meet? Are your relationships fulfilling, or do you feel tired and fatigued at the end of the day? Do you need a drink now and then to take the edge off? Do you grab for a cigarette to ease the tension? Do you feel anxious or become easily excited in social situations? Do you stay glued to the television because you find it more relaxing than interacting with others?

These examples are an indication of various acts that many of us feel the need to use in order to ease the tension in life. There's no getting around it. *The act must go!* Unfortunately, many of us feel the need for these acts to support our unstable condition, and the more we put on an act, the more we identify with the role. Because of this we lose touch with our true self and become dependent on our act. In fact, we become so attached to the act that we believe the role portrays our true identity. As a result, we become nothing more than an actor on the planet Earth in a play called Life.

It's quite amazing how we accept these performances and the characters we portray as though they are real. If you observe closely, you will see how we have learned to put on an act in place of who we are and how we really feel. It's similar to being at a masquerade party where the charade never ends and the masks never come off. So, the masquerade goes on and on, separating us further from who we really are and dividing us from one another.

YOU'RE PERFECT THE WAY YOU ARE

Regardless of whether or not you think you're perfect, you are perfect just as you are. You see, something is perfect when it's exactly the way it is, and that does not mean the way you or anyone else thinks something should be. The reason you don't see it that way is your idea of perfection or the *right way* to act influences your judgment. Unfortunately, with those ideas come feelings of uncertainty. As a result, you are often in a self-perpetuating state of confusion in an attempt to find yourself.

Life as we know it is an evolutionary process of expansion and growth. This constant change means all of us are moving into the unknown at every moment of our lives. Consequently, you can't know who you are—*you can only be who you are*—and that's a spontaneous expression that comes out of relationship. So stop trying and start being.

Ask yourself why this paranoid game goes on among us and why we accept it this way. Surely it's no secret that most people on this planet are tense and uncertain of themselves. Once you realize that, you can drop the act because you won't be worried or embarrassed about how you look to others. *It just won't matter anymore.*

Of course, being yourself is no different from being who you already are. The only difference is that, when you accept who you are, it no longer matters what people think of you. Consequently, you can let go and enjoy yourself at all times no matter where you are or whom you are with.

~

LET GO
OF YOUR FEAR
OF NOT BEING PERFECT,
AND YOU CAN STOP ACTING
LIKE WHO YOU THINK YOU SHOULD BE,
AND START BEING WHO
YOU REALLY
ARE.

~

CHAPTER 11

SUCCESS AND FAILURE

Macbeth: " If we should fail-
Lady Macbeth: We fail! /
But screw your courage to the sticking place, /
And we'll not fail."

William Shakespeare

If you're like most people, you have ideas and beliefs about success and failure, and whether you realize it or not, those mind-thoughts influence the outcome of events in your life. This chapter will focus on the type of thoughts you have that prevent you from getting the results you want.

NO SUCH THING AS FAILURE

There is no such thing as failure, only different results brought about by your actions. The truth is, you can't fail at anything you do because, in order to fail, your actions would have to have no results and that's impossible. The important thing to remember is the result you get, whatever it may be, makes you successful because you created it.

The question, then, is not whether you are successful, but whether you are creating the results you want. If the answer is no, you'll be happy to find out the power to produce the results you're looking for lies within you.

STAYING FOCUSED

To perform to the best of your ability, you can't get upset over the outcome of events. You mustn't allow yourself to become distracted. You must remain focused at all times with an uninterrupted vision of the desired outcome. That means not blaming others and taking responsibility for the outcome of events. Never forget that you are responsible for creating the results you get. In fact, you want responsibility for the results; otherwise, you give up the power to create the results you want by inadvertently empowering others with control over the outcome of events in your life.

Remain open-minded. If at first you don't succeed, try different ways to get the results you're looking for, and remember that *any result you get is a learning opportunity that brings you one step closer to the result you're looking for*. So don't waste time trying the same thing over and over again if it doesn't work.

∼

THE WORST MISTAKE A PERSON CAN MAKE
IS ONE THAT TEACHES HIM NOTHING.

∼

Keep in mind that even laboratory mice in a maze stop going down the same path after two or three times when they don't find the cheese. One more thing mice don't do: they don't waste time thinking about how difficult it will be to find the cheese. They just keep going until they get the desired result, more cheese.

The truth is mice don't have self-awareness with the ability to contemplate the situation. That's one reason they're so hard to get rid of. They don't give up. They don't understand failure, so they just keep trying. Humans, on the other hand, using the power of mind, can create anything from obstacles on the path to an unobstructed view of the goal. Unfortunately, most people create obstacles.

IT'S AS DIFFICULT AS YOU MAKE IT

As a result of difficulties experienced in the past and observations of others struggling for success, you most likely acquired a set of beliefs about what it takes to be successful. Consequently, believing that struggling is necessary to succeed makes it so. Stop for a moment and ask yourself if you believe it's just as easy to succeed as it is to fail. If you're like most people, you believe that being successful is difficult, and you need luck and arduous work to succeed. *Not so!* In fact, it's easier to succeed than it is to fail because the life force inherent in all things is continually moving you toward expansion and completion of your goals.

In order to be successful you must embody the idea of success, remain dedicated to achieving your goal, do the very best that you can, and at the same time, be unattached to the outcome. In other words, stay out of your own way so that you don't inhibit the process you've put in motion. Once you visualize success, forget about being successful or worrying about failure. Continue with the knowledge that your idea will move you toward completion of your goals.

~

IT'S YOUR BELIEF
THAT IT'S HARDER TO BE
SUCCESSFUL AND EASIER TO FAIL
THAT KEEPS YOU RUNNING FROM FAILURE
AND STRUGGLING FOR SUCCESS.

~

THE DESIRE FOR SUCCESS

It's your desire to attain success that makes your journey a difficult one. These desires turn into needs, making fulfillment of those needs your purpose. Thinking this way puts you on a level of survival, making every day you work toward those goals a desperate one. Life itself is then experienced as a burden, while success is viewed as a relief from the struggle. The problem with this kind of thinking is that once you have completed your goal and have satisfied your needs, you're back where you started, struggling to reach the next goal to fulfill your desire once again.

~

WHEN MEETING YOUR GOALS BECOMES
NECESSARY IN ORDER TO BE HAPPY,
YOU CAN BET THAT HAPPINESS
WILL ALWAYS BE ONE
STEP AWAY.

~

FEAR OF FAILURE

When you're not successful at achieving your goals, ask yourself, "What am I feeling about failing?" Keep in mind there is no reason to rationalize or hide the truth about your feelings since not getting the results you want has already disclosed that you have ideas that caused you to fail. Remember, what you think about success or failure is already reflected in your results. Therefore, this self-inquiry is not asked to determine whether you have ideas and beliefs that inhibit you from reaching your goal; that is self-evident in the outcome of events. Rather the purpose of this inquiry is for you to get in touch with the thoughts and feelings you have that are causing unwanted results.

By bringing your feelings to the surface and disclosing the thoughts associated with them, you can be free of their effect. You'll no longer think of yourself as a failure. You will know the reason you're not getting the result you want is because of your ideas, your beliefs, and your fears. This may sound too easy. However, by exposing these thoughts as the cause of unwanted results, they no longer have power over you. Having cleared the path to success, you are free to create the results you're looking for.

To deny your true feelings and the thoughts associated with them is tantamount to sentencing yourself to a life of dissatisfaction and despair. This is an opportune time for you to be honest with yourself about your feelings. After all, what have you got to lose besides that which has held you back up till now?

TRUE SUCCESS

I'm sure you've heard of people who are successful, but in pursuing their goals, have little if any regard for others. Are those people really happy with their achievements? Are they enjoying themselves while working toward accomplishing their goals? In most cases the answer is no. You can't be happy if your goal is to satisfy your needs and your needs alone. In other words, if your purpose in life is merely to serve yourself, you will never feel fulfilled, nor will you be satisfied with what you have.

~

GIVE UP
ALL YOUR REASONS
FOR WANTING SUCCESS,
AND NOT ONLY WILL YOU BE SUCCESSFUL,
BUT YOU'LL ALSO BE ABLE TO ENJOY IT.

~

The most important thing about being successful isn't getting what you want. It's about considering others as well as yourself and getting satisfaction from what you've accomplished while you're accomplishing it. If you think otherwise, you may end up with what you want, but you won't be able to enjoy it.

~

IF YOU
WOULD LET GO
OF YOUR REASONS
FOR WANTING SUCCESS,
YOU COULD BE SUCCESSFUL
WHENEVER YOU WANTED.
UNTIL THAT TIME,
YOU GET TO EXPERIENCE FAILURE
BECAUSE OF YOUR REASONS
FOR WANTING
SUCCESS.

~

Chapter 12

Overcoming Fear and Uncertainty

*"No passion so effectually robs the mind
of all its power of acting and reasoning as fear."*

Edmund Burke

Much of the discomfort we experience in our relationships comes from our fear of expressing our true feelings. We have concerns about what we should or shouldn't say and how we should say it. By thinking this way, we tailor our conversations, affecting our ability to communicate openly and honestly.

We all have feelings that arise when we're speaking with others, and with those feelings we influence our relationships. For example, if you feel that others are looking at you as though you're inadequate, chances are they're looking at you that way because that's how you see yourself. The response you get is directly related to your thoughts about yourself.

Most of us are caught up in this cause and effect process that controls our lives. Take notice of how we avoid direct eye contact in conversation. One person looks away to ease his or her discomfort, and the other person sensing it, also looks away. Another example occurs when you want to approach someone to say hello but you're so nervous that you don't follow through. Another instance of avoidance happens when you want to tell someone you love him or her but you can't find the courage to say the words. These moments can be so uncomfortable that we try desperately to avoid them.

We're continually getting bounced around by the cause and effect process we set in motion, allowing fear to suppress our true feelings and free self-expression. But what exactly is it that we are trying to avoid? It's the experience of our own self! That's right. It may look as though we are trying to avoid the person we're speaking to, but actually we're avoiding our feelings. In truth, we are trying to avoid the things we dislike, are uncertain of, and are unwilling to accept about ourselves, that stand between us and the person we're in a relationship with.

LIMITATIONS AND BREAKING THROUGH THEM

When you tense up, finding it difficult to say or do the things you would like to, that's the perfect time to do those things you're avoiding. After all, what could you possibly lose that's worth sacrificing your true feelings? No matter what the outcome, you and those around you will benefit from this direct approach.

.e a decision *right now* to stop wasting time feeling threatened and insecure. Make a commitment to yourself to do those things you would like but haven't had the courage to do.

Facing your fears with this head-on approach is the quickest way to free yourself of them. However, you must have a passion for life and a yearning for liberation since without them you will not find the courage to face your fears. If at first your fears get the best of you, don't be discouraged. Don't give up because you think you can't succeed. Giving up is just another way of avoiding your fears once again. Look for and begin to see this avoidance that blocks your true feelings and free self-expression. Remember, with commitment you can and will break through.

∼

YOU

CAN'T GO

FROM HERE TO THERE

UNTIL YOU KNOW WHERE HERE IS.

TO MOVE AHEAD,

ACCEPT WHERE

YOU ARE.

∼

OVERCOMING FEAR

You can overcome your fears in a number of ways. One way is to stop worrying about them. I realize this sounds a bit trite, but it really works. By not thinking about things that instill fear, you stop programming those thoughts into your mind. Another way to free yourself is to pay such close attention to what you are doing that you don't allow negative thoughts to enter into your consciousness. Or you can take the direct approach by accepting yourself as you are and facing your fears head on. This direct approach is a powerful tool to overcoming your fears because it's your resistance to fear that gives it power over you. Consequently, your fears and the experiences associated with them give you the biggest opportunity to free yourself from the effects of fear.

Each approach allows you to diffuse your fears and gain power over them. So take this opportunity to free yourself from the effect of your fears rather than trying to avoid them.

~

IF
YOU
WOULD ACCEPT WHAT
YOU DON'T WANT TO EXPERIENCE,
YOU WOULDN'T HAVE TO EXPERIENCE IT,
BECAUSE
WHAT YOU DON'T WANT TO ACCEPT
IS EXACTLY WHAT
YOU GET.

~

BELIEVING THE LIE

Programmed for so long, you actually believe these self-imposed limitations are a part of your identity. They're not, so open yourself to the possibility that all of your fears and limitations are nothing more than unnecessary baggage you carry around with you. Upon realizing the truth and the absurdity of what you have done to restrict yourself, you will be able to laugh at your foolishness and you will be free from the limitations you have imposed on yourself.

~

BY
HOLDING ON
TO YOUR BELIEF
THAT THINGS WILL BE
THE WAY YOU REMEMBER THEM,
THEY WILL.

IT
DOESN'T
HAVE TO BE THAT WAY,
SO DON'T BELIEVE IT.

~

CHAPTER 13

INTEGRITY AND
BUILDING CHARACTER

*"There is only one corner of the universe
you can be certain of improving,
and that's your own self."*

Aldous Huxley

Unwilling to accept what arises, we tend to look at life as an unwanted responsibility. From this negative point of view, we take all of the positive things in our lives for granted, never appreciating what we have or the wonderment of it all. This adolescent attitude with its need for satisfaction causes most of us to try to make life work *our way* rather than accepting what is. Not liking or wanting to deal with our reality, we attempt to avoid it. This avoidance leads us to common adolescent traits, for example, laziness and a reluctance to accept responsibilities.

Being irresponsible can involve contradicting ourselves and then rationalizing our actions. In fact, we'll do almost anything to get our way or to avoid what we don't want to do. The desire to have everything our way can be so strong that we'll go so far as to break our agreements. It's obvious that to live in harmony with one another, we must keep our agreements. Unfortunately, as a result of our childlike disposition, we tend to break agreements rather easily.

By breaking an agreement, you may get what you want, but you lose much more. Your word is your bond. When you break your word, others lose faith in you, and more importantly, you lose faith in yourself. You shatter your own character, ultimately losing respect for yourself. From that point on, the words you speak have no power, causing those words to be heard as though spoken from an irresponsible fool, to whom only fools will listen.

～

SAY

WHAT YOU MEAN

AND DO WHAT YOU SAY,

AND DON'T DO TO OTHERS

WHAT YOU WOULDN'T HAVE OTHERS

DO TO YOU.

～

GROWING UP

To understand how you acquired these adolescent traits, think back to your youth. As a child, you knew what you wanted and became upset when you didn't

get it. As time went on, you developed certain personality traits that you used to get your way. You may have
agreed to something you had no intention of doing just
to end the conversation, or you would become angry
and confrontational in an attempt to win your argu-
ment.

While you were busy figuring out how to manipulate your parents, they were busy trying to teach you
how to survive. Little by little the responsibility of survival was imposed on you and quickly became overwhelming. From then on, life started to look like an
unwanted burden.

This outlook causes us to seek help and comfort
from others through what we view as the turbulent
voyage of life. For instance, an adult male may look for
a wife who reminds him of his parent, someone who
will comfort him the way his mother did. A woman
may look for security in a father figure—a dependable
man who will always be there to assure her.

We all have responsibilities, and you may be trying
to avoid yours by looking to others for help the same
way you ran to your mother or father when you needed
help as a child. It takes a mature person to let go of his
or her fears and selfish desires, something a child is unwilling to do. If you're still holding onto yours, the
odds are you're struggling as an adult. In fact, you're
probably so busy trying to control everything in your

life that it never occurred to you to question whether there could be a better way.

Accepting responsibility means taking responsibility for everything we think, say, and do. Once you realize the high price you pay for every irresponsible act and take full responsibility for it, you can be a powerful force in the world. So, what will it be? The choice is yours once more.

~

REMEMBER:
YOU ARE ONLY AS GOOD AS YOUR WORD,
AND YOUR CHARACTER SHINES
THROUGH YOUR EXAMPLE.

~

CHAPTER 14

BEING TRUE TO YOURSELF

"This above all: to thine own self be true . . ."

William Shakespeare

In many situations we may find it easier to rationalize and ignore our conscience in order to justify doing what we want. The reason is that honesty doesn't always allow us to have things our way. Unfortunately, ignoring our true feelings to satisfy personal desires has a negative impact on our lives.

By ignoring these thoughts and their associated feelings, they get suppressed, causing unnecessary pain and suffering. This self-inflicted suffering can take many forms like tension and anxiety, upset and despair, self-sabotage or physical illness.

To be free of these self-imposed limitations, you must be honest with yourself about doing the right thing. However, doing the right thing is not a matter of emulating others, but rather doing what you know and feel in your heart is right. There is no healthy alternative to honesty since acting on thoughts that derive from your mind and not from your heart negatively impacts your life.

～

IT'S NOT
WHAT YOU DO THAT MATTERS,
BUT WHY YOU DO IT
AND
WHY YOU DON'T.

～

KNOWING RIGHT FROM WRONG

It's safe to say that everyone knows right from wrong. You know you shouldn't lie, cheat, steal, or cause physical harm to others. But what about less egregious acts that you rationalize and do anyway? For example, have you ever been in a special relationship but in a very subtle way flirted with another person? Nothing blatant, but flirting just the same. You may say this kind of behavior is acceptable since it's innocent and you have no intention of following through. But ask yourself, would you be acting the same way if your significant other were observing you? What about lunch or drinks after work with someone you've been admiring? It sounds innocent enough. But what if your significant other saw you and overheard your conversation? Would you feel uncomfortable in the situation? If the answer is yes, then you know these kinds of flirtations are wrong.

What about those times you talk about someone when he or she is not present? If you wouldn't say those same words in the presence of that person, you can be sure it's the wrong thing to say. Another example is getting too much change back from a purchase and rationalizing that it's all right to keep it because the service was bad or the price was too high. The list is endless, but I'm sure you get the idea.

Most of us are masters at deceiving ourselves and rationalizing anything if it gets us what we want. In light of this, when asking yourself how you really feel about something, you must be committed to accepting the truth rather than your version of it. This is where integrity comes in. You must be willing to take a hard look at yourself and admit to what you see, and if what you see doesn't feel right, you have to change it.

You must give up your old ways once you realize there is something in you that's saying those ways are not right for you or for the people around you. It comes right down to abiding by your innermost feelings and listening to that intuitive voice inside. It's admitting that what you're doing is harmful to you and to others and that stopping this kind of behavior is essential.

~

THE
TRUTH IS NEVER
DIFFICULT TO FIND
UNLESS YOU'RE UNWILLING
TO FACE IT.

~

AVOIDING THE TRUTH

It's imperative for you to know the negative effect of avoiding your innermost feelings. To disregard your thoughts and the feelings associated with them, you have to put those thoughts out of your mind. You must find a place to hide them, and the only place you can conceal those thoughts is your *subconscious*—a dark place in your mind, a crypt where you can store your demons and all is forgotten. Unfortunately, escaping the effects of these thoughts is impossible. Even worse, by maintaining this subconscious storage space, you give up the use of a portion of your consciousness. This limits your consciousness, leaving you with inadequate resources to realize your true potential.

It's easy to see why so many people are walking around in an unconscious state and why there's a lack of insight into our problems, causing confusion, anger, and fear leading to conflict. In order to free yourself from this condition, you have to give up personality traits based on power, greed, and survival. You must be honest with yourself. You must have ethics and integrity. In other words, you must express the love that is inherent within you.

Once you commit to stopping the behavior that compromises what you know is right, you must hold your ground without turning back. This may sound like a ploy to get you to do the right thing, but with a guilty conscience, you lose respect for yourself and others lose respect for you as well. Consequently, you carry feelings of inadequacy with you wherever you go, limiting the dynamics of your personality. What a high price to pay for mediocrity!

~

YOU
CAN'T EXPECT
TO FIND THE TRUTH
IF THE TRUTH ISN'T MORE
IMPORTANT TO YOU THAN
FULFILLING YOUR PERSONAL DESIRES.
UNTIL THEN, YOU WILL SPEND ALL
OF YOUR TIME IN RELENTLESS
PURSUIT OF SATISFACTION
AND FULFILLMENT.

~

CHAPTER 15

YOUR MIND:
SERVANT OR MASTER

*"It is the mind that maketh good or ill,
That maketh wretch or happy,
rich or poor."*

Edmund Spenser

The mind serves as a memory bank. With your mind's ability to recall information, you manage your way through life remembering where you live, what direction to take to get to work, or how to drive a car. This ability to remember can also be a limiting factor. Rather than helping, the ability to draw on memories can enslave you as well.

For example, when you experience something, the details are recorded in your memory. From that memory, you draw the conclusion that you *know* what something is like. Consequently, your belief is that the experience is gospel and the only way it could be, and as a result, *your experience never changes*. In other words, by holding onto the way something was, you cause that occurrence to be experienced the same way over and over again. Thus you remain at the affect of your beliefs with no apparent way out, never realizing that your thoughts give birth to the experiences that enslave you. Simply stated, *your experiences in life are a reflection of your ideas and your beliefs.*

~

FROM YOUR EXPERIENCES
YOU FORMULATE CONCLUSIONS AND BELIEFS,
AND FROM THOSE BELIEFS
YOU CREATE YOUR EXPERIENCES.

~

If you followed this creative process of the mind, you now have the knowledge necessary to free yourself from the thoughts that hold you back and the experiences associated with them. You may also begin to realize that there is no limitation to what you can do; actually, there never was, except for the limitations you imposed upon yourself. Therefore, you don't have to worry about the future, nor would you want to because those thoughts will reflect themselves into your life. *Ultimately, you are free, right here and now, to create your life experience any way you choose.* So why not choose to create a reality that works, rather than one that doesn't?

A NEW BEGINNING

It's quite an eye-opener to realize that thoughts are creative, and, when linked to our beliefs, they run our lives. Of course, it's one thing to intellectually understand this and quite another to live a life free of the mind's influence. Unfortunately, conditioning runs deep. Throughout life, our experiences have always validated our beliefs; and it's no wonder, since our beliefs create our experiences.

~

STAND STRONG
WHILE FACING YOUR CREATION,
KNOWING IT AS A PASSING MOMENT
AND A REFLECTION OF YOUR MIND
THAT IS NOT TO BE BELIEVED
BUT SIMPLY EXPERIENCED
AND FORGOTTEN.

~

From past experiences, we draw conclusions and beliefs. Operating from those ideas, we create our reality. Consequently, the kinds of thoughts one has determine the kinds of experiences that take place in one's life. Therefore, *what we believe to be true about ourselves and about the way things are is exactly how it will be for us.*

The mind has unlimited creative potential that man has not yet mastered. Instead, man, through his own ignorance, has allowed his mind to master him.

~

IF
YOU BELIEVE
WHAT YOU EXPERIENCED
YESTERDAY CAN'T CHANGE,
IT WILL BE YOUR EXPERIENCE TOMORROW.

DON'T BELIEVE YOUR EXPERIENCE,
JUST EXPERIENCE IT.

~

CHAPTER 16

THE SEARCH FOR AN
ILLUSIVE GOAL

*"Which of you by taking thought
can add one cubit unto his stature."*

Jesus Christ

It is meaningless to search for what we already have and to strive for that which we already are. Although our quest to find fulfillment through external means goes on in vain, we continue to search outside ourselves for something that will help us improve the quality of our lives. In pursuit of the answer, we pick up beliefs about what it takes to reach our goal, and those ideas become self-imposed obstacles on our path.

~

IT'S ONLY WHEN YOUR SEARCH ON THE PATH
HAS BROUGHT YOU TO THE THRESHOLD
THAT YOU MUST GIVE UP THE QUEST
FOR THE VERY GOAL ITSELF.
OTHERWISE, YOUR GOAL
WILL ALWAYS BE
SOMETHING
DISTANT
FROM
YOU.

~

The truth is, as long as you have an idea about finding inner peace you will never find it. The reason is that peace of mind doesn't exist within the confines of your mind, but rather, it exists prior to mind, in a space clear and unobstructed by thought. Consequently, to experience inner peace you must give up your idea about it.

It's that simple, and the reason it's so simple is that you already possess the power to transform the quality of your life, but rather than using that power for self-improvement, you continue to limit yourself with it.

TRAVELING THE PATH

You alone hold the key to the door that stands between you and all that you are seeking. The key is not to follow your beliefs or anyone else's but to seek the truth from within and to follow a path of the heart. Love yourself for who you really are. If you become aware of something about yourself that seems impossible to love, make a commitment to change your behavior, and the door that stands between you and your aspirations will open wide.

～

IF

YOU

WOULD STOP

SEARCHING FOR THE GOAL,

YOU COULD EXPERIENCE IT.

HAVING EXPERIENCED IT, THE THOUGHT

OF NEEDING SOMETHING MORE

WOULD NEVER ENTER

YOUR MIND.

～

You are the way. You don't have to wait to get there because you are already there. An enlightened person is simply someone who found out!

~

SEARCHING
TO FIND YOUR TRUE SELF
IS LIKE SEARCHING FOR AIR
WHEN YOU'VE BEEN BREATHING IT
ALL YOUR LIFE.

WELCOME HOME!

~

CHAPTER 17

WHY YOUR LIFE
IS THE WAY IT IS

*"We do not see things as they are,
but as we are."*

The Talmud

111

Most of us are caught up in a self-perpetuating state of cause and effect. In order to see the whole picture with you as the writer, director, and actor, you must explore the process of creative consciousness and the laws that govern it. To understand this process, focus your attention on the *cause* of your experiences rather than the *effect*.

Without realizing that we are the cause of what occurs in our lives, we believe the things that happen to us are out of our control. This conclusion has us asking questions such as "She was such a nice person. Why did it happen to her?" or, "Why is my life so difficult? Why me? If there really is a God, why does He allow all this suffering to go on, and why doesn't He help us?"

The answers to these questions can be found in the creative process of the mind. Once this process is understood, we regain our natural ability to intentionally create our life experiences the way we envision them. Actually, creating our life experiences is nothing new. We've always been responsible for creating everything we experience in our lives. The only problem is we are creating from random, rather than intentional, thoughts.

Our lack of knowledge about the creative process keeps us under the illusion that we are at the mercy of some unknown creator who rules over our destiny. In truth, *you are the creator and the created*. Don't be mistaken. I'm not implying there isn't a higher intelligence or God, but I am suggesting that you are not, nor have you ever been, separate and apart from it.

As an integral part of the creative process and the principles behind it, we are subject to its laws, giving us the power to create as well as destroy. Consequently, our personal situation and the state of this planet are the result of the way we are choosing to use this power.

~

BE

AWARE

OF EVERY

THOUGHT YOU HAVE

BECAUSE THOSE THOUGHTS

WILL TAKE YOU ON A JOURNEY

WHETHER YOU WANT TO GO THERE OR NOT.

~

THE CREATIVE PROCESS

Think of your mind as a movie camera loaded with film. The negatives or imprints on each frame are your mind-thoughts, that is, your ideas about yourself, the world, and the entire universe. Think of the projection screen as a mirror. When you look into the mirror, what you see is a reflection of those mind-thoughts. Only now it appears as though you walked into the mirror, and your thoughts are projected in three-dimensional forms like that of a hologram.

In other words, the body you identify yourself with is now enveloped within the conceptualization of your self which encompasses the universe and all it contains. What you see "out there" is no different from who and what you are; however, by identifying yourself with your body, you believe you are separate from

114

that which you see around you. In actuality it's all one Self expressed as an idea in various forms. When you look into the mirror, what you see, and your experience of it, is relative to your point of view. That viewing point is directly related to your level of consciousness and your knowledge of the Self. One could say everything you come in contact with is an expression of yourself, and that your experience of the Self depends on what you think you are.

It is important to remember that mind-thoughts have a life of their own, and with every thought a process is set in motion. The laws of electromagnetism govern this process and work like this: mind-thoughts emit electromagnetically charged waves of energy. These waves of energy have polarity with energy of equal and opposite charge. This means one's mind-thoughts are attracted to something, and that something is the experience associated with the corresponding thought.

Because mind-thoughts have a natural affinity for their counterpart, every thought has the potential to manifest into a physical reality. So from now on, if you find yourself in an unwanted situation, don't forget that your thoughts brought it about. If this explanation of the relationship between mind-thoughts and your life experiences is too abstract to follow, then simply remember this: *what you think is what you get.*

When you understand your relationship to all

things, you will realize how senseless it is to complain about the way things are because you're creating it that way. Furthermore, it becomes obvious that we, the human race, have created a world of pain and suffering where it need not exist.

GETTING THE CREATIVE PROCESS
TO WORK FOR YOU

If your life isn't working, you have issues to deal with. Your ideas and beliefs are causing problems in your life that need to be addressed. Why wait any longer when all that is necessary to discover these limiting thoughts is for you to look at your life experiences? That's right! Look at what is taking place in your life. Those experiences will reveal the kinds of thoughts you're having because your experiences are a reflection of your thoughts. Once those thoughts are revealed and acknowledged, you can improve the quality of your life by letting go of negative thoughts.

In other words, you can take affirmative action. You can change the way things are by creating what you want. All that's necessary is for you to choose what you want in life and then push yourself if necessary to obtain it. There's nothing mystical about it. If you want to create something in your life, you're the only one who can do it because the creative power is within you.

There is one more thing you should know about

the creative process and that is it works much better if what you want to create comes from your heart.

Knowledge of the creative process and how it works should give you a deeper understanding of why your life is the way it is. Having this knowledge should also give you insight into the true meaning of sayings like, "Fear the wrath of God" or, "I'm a God-fearing man." In other words, God is not the one to fear since in this case God turns out to be you or *the creative power within you*. So if you have anything at all to fear, it's yourself or the way you use this God-given power. With that in mind, from this day forward, may God bless and guide you in the way you choose to use this power.

~

IF
EVERYTHING
YOU SEE AND EXPERIENCE
IS A PRODUCT OF WHAT YOU BELIEVE
ABOUT YOURSELF AND YOUR POINT OF VIEW,
THEN THE POSSIBILITIES ARE UNLIMITED.

WHAT A WONDERFUL
OPPORTUNITY LIES AHEAD!
TAKE ADVANTAGE OF IT,
IT'S YOURS.

~

CHAPTER 18

LIVING OUTSIDE THE CONFINES OF YOUR MIND

*"The only way to discover
the limits of the possible
is to go beyond to the impossible."*

Arthur C. Clarke

Memories influence all of our experiences. Our memories dictate what we think, say, and do, our likes and dislikes, and all of our choices. For example, most of the choices we make are nothing more than decisions influenced by our past. The reason for this is the choices we make are never prior to our mind-thoughts. Our tendency is to stop and think about making a choice before we make it. Consequently, by depending on memory to make decisions, we are influenced by our past. It may appear as though we are operating in the present, but as long as memory influences us, we're operating within the confines of our minds.

THE PRICE YOU PAY

Operating from memory and out of touch with our intuitive nature, we lose faith in our ability to make correct, spontaneous choices. Because of this uncertainty and lack of faith in ourselves, we revert to what we know and are comfortable with, resulting in a dependency on memory and rational thinking to get by. Victims of a limited mind held captive by fears of the unknown, we become nothing more than robots functioning at the mercy of our programming.

Using memory to make decisions for the future causes us to make the wrong choices in life. For example, when deciding about what to eat, you most likely compare your experiences of food from the past in order to make your decision. The problem with depending on a thought process to make this decision is that your body may require one type of nutrition, but for one reason or another you choose something else. In other words, your mind-thoughts take you in the wrong direction.

Unfortunately, influence from the past doesn't stop there because your memory alters all of your experiences. For example, upon tasting your food, if it meets with your approval, you think it's good. But "good" relative to what? You see, in order for you to distinguish something as good or bad, you must go back in time to draw on past experiences. The fact is, the only way you can experience something as being good or bad is if you're judging it, and you can't judge something unless you're comparing it to something else. This being the case, you can't see or experience anything as it is because you're always coming from the past and looking through a veil of memories which modifies all of your experiences.

The implications of the influence that memory has over us are staggering. Apparently, your mind influences every aspect of your life, meaning you've never experienced reality, just your idea of it. That idea begets another idea, which influences your next experience and so on. Living this way, you can't appreciate anything for what it is because you never experience *what is.*

Operating at this level, you stunt your growth because you repeat the same experiences over and over again. Your experiences may appear to be different from one another, but they are nothing more than events influenced by memories of your past. Now I ask you, is living in the past to make decisions for the future really living at all? Stop for a moment and contemplate the magnitude of the mind's influence over you. If you're honest with yourself, you will realize that what you call living is nothing more than existing. Congratulations! You're beginning to see past the illusion of a programmed reality.

CUTTING LOOSE

Free self-expression unencumbered by the past comes only when the actions you take are spontaneous and not derived from contemplation and comparison. In other words, true creative living, which is the freedom to express one's real Self and true nature, comes only when you express yourself prior to the thought process.

To accomplish this, you must have trust and be willing to express yourself spontaneously. Then and only then can you be free of the past and the mind's influence over you. You can begin living your life with enthusiasm and anticipation rather than living with fear and uncertainty. This radical way of living becomes an effortless flow of creative self-expression as you become liberated from your past. Living outside the confines of your mind is like nothing you've ever experienced, so get ready for the experience of your life!

~

WHY
DECIDE
ON WHAT TO DO
WHEN YOU CAN TRUST YOURSELF
TO DO IT FOR YOU?

~

CHAPTER 19

COMMUNING WITH NATURE

"Nature is but a name for an effect,
Whose cause is God."

William Cowper

On a clear, sunny day, take a walk alone in a park or a wooded area. Watch the animals. Experience the earth and the trees around you. Go to a lake, a river, or the ocean and sit quietly by the water's edge. Still your mind. Remain silent and take it all in. Slow down, take a deep breath, and give yourself the opportunity to enjoy what nature has to offer. Don't overlook the natural beauty that surrounds you. Get in touch with it. Don't make nature something foreign to you; it's a part of you, not something to be viewed from afar. By closely observing nature, you can fall into harmony with it. A calm and nurturing experience can be found in nature if you give yourself the time to find it.

Try feeding the birds and the squirrels in a park. Get close enough to them to look into their eyes. You'll notice their eyes are sharp and focused, and they don't appear to be thinking about anything. Animals are not worrying about where their next meal is coming from or what they're supposed to do next. They just do what they have to do. They don't run around frantically and if they are running around, usually they're playing with one another.

Animals are focused and alert. They operate in the present, not in their minds. They're *being*, not trying to figure out how or what to be. They're just being. If you're asking yourself how animals manage to operate in the present, you're asking the wrong question. They just do it. That's the difference. Animals don't contemplate something before they act. They don't think about how difficult something could be because they're too busy doing it. Animals are spontaneous and simply go for it.

What do you think would happen to a squirrel being chased by a dog if the squirrel stopped first to contemplate its escape? It would be the end of that squirrel. A squirrel doesn't stop to think about what to do. Instead, in a flash, it's gone up the nearest tree. It all happens so fast there isn't a moment to think.

Could you imagine the confusion that would take place if all wildlife and vegetation had to think about survival? The balance of nature would be thrown off while all life stopped to figure out its next move. The result would be something like the way we have it now: a constant struggle to survive causing an imbalance affecting all aspects of life.

The truth is no imbalance really exists, not in nature, natural resources, air quality, the ozone layer, mental or physical health, or for that matter in anything other than the imbalance we humans have created for ourselves. Fortunately, we are unable to throw the consciousness of animals off balance, so animals in nature remain a stabilizing force in our lives.

Infants are another example of a stabilizing force. Have you noticed the feeling you get when you look into an infant's eyes? You become entranced by their presence. Why do you suppose that phenomenon occurs? It's simple. Their minds clear, infants are operating in the present. And that's a very powerful place to be. Focusing on an individual who is operating in the present can transport people out of their body consciousness and into an experience of their inner being.

Since all things in nature operate in the present, we can benefit from interacting with nature. Consequently, paying close attention to any living thing that is in balance can bring us into harmony with it. Examples of this phenomenon exist all around us, and we can experience this nurturing quality if we allow ourselves to be open to it. All we have to do is slow down and take the time to experience it.

~

IF
AT TIMES
LIFE IS TOO
MUCH TO DEAL WITH,
COMMUNING WITH NATURE
CAN BRIDGE THE GAP
BETWEEN THE WAY
YOU THINK IT IS
AND THE WAY
IT REALLY
IS.

~

CHAPTER 20

SPONTANEOUS CREATIVE COMMUNICATION

*"The two words 'information' and 'communication'
are often used interchangeably,
but they signify quite different things.
Information is giving out;
communication is getting through."*

Sydney J. Harris

Most of us do not experience the freedom of creative self-expression because our ability to communicate is impaired. Basically, our communication with others consists of controlled responses which are rarely, if ever, on a creative level. We're usually stuck in dull, thought-out conversations, expressing nothing more than what we think, rather than what comes up for us spontaneously.

I'm not suggesting that you run around blurting out everything that comes to mind; that would be nothing more than expressing your reaction to something. What I am suggesting is that you can reach a level of communication free of distortion and controlled responses. By letting go and getting out of your own way, you can free yourself of the mind's conditioning and its self-imposed restraints.

Expressing yourself in this way, you regain your

spontaneity and your enthusiasm for life itself. At that level, communication is no longer limited to an experience of individuality and separateness, but rather evolves to a spontaneous experience created out of relationship.

In order to achieve a level of spontaneous creative communication, you must be willing to express yourself openly and honestly. Creative communication isn't about expressing what you *think* you should say; it's saying what comes up for you spontaneously. You simply go with the flow.

Unfortunately, most of us have conformed to a set of social standards consisting of guidelines that restrict us—a set of unspoken agreements not to say the wrong thing or go beyond a certain point. Our communication is usually filtered through layers of mind stuff and carefully thought out—something clever perhaps—but never creative and outside the confines of the mind. By operating that way, we endeavor not to make the mistake of saying the wrong thing exposing ourselves to ridicule and attack.

To listen to our conversations, you would never know we are creative beings. We rarely let go and express what comes up for us, that is, of course, unless we're so angry that we feel the need to relieve our frustration. At best, that's nothing more than expressing our emotions and acting out at someone else's expense. For the most part, we rarely express ourselves on a

creative level because most of what we say is a condi-
tioned response. In view of this conditioning, we never
experience spontaneous creative communication—the
expression of our real Self and true nature.

TUNING IN

By paying close attention to the person you're in relationship with, you cut through the mind stuff that influences your communication. You tune into the experience taking place with such intense concentration
that you leave absolutely no space in your mind for ex-
traneous thoughts or judgments to enter.

You must be willing to put out all you've got. Stay
alert and aware, or you will fall back into the influence
of your mind. You must be spontaneous, never letting
your mind wander off the present experience, not even
for a second. If you do, you will fall outside of the here
and now, out of the moment, and into an imaginary
space where your mind can wander off in a daydream.

While communicating, maintain contact by looking into a person's eyes. Making eye contact doesn't
mean you try to stare a person down. You simply focus
your attention on the person you're speaking with.
Watch and listen with such intensity that you are not
aware of stray thoughts. In other words, *be in the
present at every moment*. The instant you catch your
mind wandering or thinking about what you're saying
rather than saying it, tune back in. With passion,

giving it all you've got, focus your attention on exactly what is taking place and not your idea or your feelings about it. Just what is, and nothing more.

You are a creative self-expression. Why try to change what you are into a controlled response? Learn to express yourself spontaneously. Continue this process with relentless pursuit. Regain your natural ability to express yourself openly and honestly with enthusiasm. Experience the joy of life inherent within you.

~

TO
EXPERIENCE
THE SPONTANEOUS EXPRESSION
OF YOUR REAL SELF AND TRUE NATURE,
IT SEEMS TO ME ALL YOU CAN DO IS BE.
AND IF ALL YOU CAN DO IS BE,
THEN ALL YOU CAN BE
IS WHO YOU
ALREADY
ARE.

~

CHAPTER 21

TOWARD THE ONE

"The world and my being,
its life and mine, were one.
The microcosm and macrocosm
were at length atoned, at length in harmony.
I lived in everything;
everything entered and lived in me."

George Macdonald

Your experience is created out of a relationship between the experiencer and the experienced, the observer and the observed. Although not apparent, your experience is not of something *out there*, independent of you the observer. You are not the subject experiencing an independent object. However, because you identify yourself with your body, your experience seems to be of something separate and apart from you, perpetuating your belief in the illusion of individuality.

This misconception keeps you from realizing there is but one consciousness or Self, expressed as both the observer and the observed, and that *your experience is the result of that union*. Furthermore, this experience does not take place in any particular location. It just is. Where it is and what it is cannot be accurately defined since anything you think about your experience separates you from it.

Your natural state is to be one with your experience, in the moment, leaving no space in your mind between the observer and the observed. You could say *experience itself is an electromagnetic moment created out of the center of polarized opposites, and out of this moment all things come into being.*

~

NOTHING
EXISTS WITHOUT
YOU, THE OBSERVER.
NO PEOPLE OR PLANET,
NOT EVEN THE UNIVERSE EXISTS
WITHOUT YOU.

IN SHORT,
WITHOUT YOUR
PARTICIPATION AS THE OBSERVER,
NOTHING EXISTS AS THE OBSERVED;
THEREFORE,
THE OBSERVER AND THE OBSERVED
MUST BE ONE AND THE SAME.

~

THE WAY

Here is a process that will assist you in cutting through the illusion of individuality and separateness.

In order to accomplish this, you will have to shift your consciousness. To begin this process, put a glass of water on a table. Sit at the table with the glass at arm's length. Focus your attention on the glass. Now pick up the glass the way you normally would, only this time watch yourself doing it. Watch as you slowly bring the glass to your mouth and take a drink. Now with the same attentiveness, slowly put the glass down on the table. Witness all of your actions as though looking not with but *through* your eyes.

Next, shift your awareness to the glass and yourself, encompassing both the observer and the observed. Now let go and merge with the experience. Focusing on the subject and the object simultaneously transcends your point of view of the experience and your interpretation of it. Free of the mind's influence, you, the experiencer, are no longer separated from the experienced. You are in the present, where all things are united as One.

～

YOU
ARE NOT THE DOER.
IT'S YOUR IDENTIFICATION
WITH THE DOER THAT LEADS YOU
TO BELIEVE YOU ARE SEPARATE AND APART
FROM YOUR EXPERIENCE RATHER
THAN BEING ONE WITH IT.

～

A DIRECT PATH

To complete this process successfully, you cannot think about doing it. Your mind must be clear and free of thought; in other words, you have to let go of any ideas about your experience in order to actually experience it. You must pay such close attention that you don't allow anything to come between you, the observer, and the observed.

If you express yourself from the heart, you can accomplish closing the gap with ease because love from the heart transcends the thoughts associated with ego. Love is also the only way for you to successfully maintain this level of consciousness for more than just fleeting moments. There's no alternative. As long as you persist in expressing what's in your head and not in your heart, you will always be separate and apart from everything around you.

**INQUIRE INTO WHO EXPERIENCES WHAT
AND BECOME ONE WITH THE ANSWER**

THE SELF
EXPERIENCE

MY SELF
EXPERIENCER

YOUR SELF
EXPERIENCED

**CONTINUE
TO BELIEVE IN WHAT YOU SEE
FROM YOUR POINT OF VIEW
AND ALL YOU WILL EXPERIENCE
IS THE ILLUSION OF TWO**

~

AFTER ALL,
WHAT IS REALITY BUT EXPERIENCE.
NOT YOURS OR MINE,
BUT SIMPLY UNQUALIFIED EXPERIENCE.

~

CHAPTER 22

THE ORIGIN OF LIFE
AND
LEARNING HOW TO LIVE

"You never enjoy the world aright,
till the sea itself floweth in your veins,
till you are clothed with the heavens,
and crowned with the stars: and perceive
yourself to be the sole heir of the whole world."

Thomas Traherne

First and foremost there is, always was, and always will be Pure Consciousness as the Source, the substratum and the ground of all Being. It is a self-generating, creative life principle consisting of pure potential, often referred to as the Self or God.

Since this creative potential consists of one undifferentiated whole of Pure Consciousness, it cannot be aware of anything, not even of being conscious. Why not? Because *Pure* Consciousness is in a state of *Being*. Not being this or that, not experiencing or being aware of anything, but simply Being. And considering Pure Consciousness is all that is, in order for it to experience anything, it must bring about a relationship with itself, for without dualism and polarity, only undifferentiated union would exist.

Pure Consciousness or the Self being a uniform whole had to make it *appear* as though there were two parts of itself. To accomplish this, it did the only thing it could do: it negated or veiled one side of itself. Partially veiled, Pure Consciousness created an *illusion* of what appeared to be a dual aspect of itself, or subjective and objective consciousness.

Now appearing as duality with the ability to reflect upon itself, Pure Consciousness possessed the ability to think. With the ability to think, this dual aspect of consciousness began to imagine the innumerable aspects of itself. At first these thoughts held in subjective consciousness manifest as energy or waves of light in an electromagnetic field (the equivalent of antimatter, spirit, or soul). The oscillation of these waves produced a distinct vibration or *sound,* a sound the Bible refers to in the beginning of creation: and God *said,* "Let there be light." It was this concentration of energy in a dense field that took the form of matter—objective consciousness—on the physical plane. (See Chapter 23, "The Reality Of Emptiness" section on quantum field theory and quantum electrodynamics).

As evolution would have it, the most developed expression of consciousness on the planet Earth is a human being. And the only thing we humans have to do to remain balanced and in good health is *be.* That's right, all we have to do to experience physical and mental well-being is to accept all of our experiences unconditionally.

This is a fundamental truth because all of our

experiences are reflections of subjective and objective consciousness. Therefore, if we avoid or resist an experience, we throw our consciousness off balance. In other words, *when you avoid or reject your experiences, you avoid and reject yourself because each of your experiences is a reflection of yourself.* There's no mistaking it; if you don't like what you get, you will continue to get what you don't like.

This dual aspect of consciousness constituting the mind is linked to solar and lunar forces through the two hemispheres of the brain; therefore, when we reject or resist any experience in our lives, an imbalance of energy occurs in and around our bodies affecting our health. This imbalance causes conditions that most of humanity suffers from: fatigue, mood swings, mental and physical disorders, and the desire to find relief.

By accepting all of our experiences, whether we like them or not, we can experience the joy and well-being that result from the perfect alignment of subjective and objective consciousness united as one. However, acceptance doesn't mean that if the roof begins to fall, you should accept it and let it clobber you or that you let the roof leak until the flow of water carries you out of the house and into the street. Accepting your experiences simply means that you accept *what is* rather than complaining, avoiding, or resisting it. And if you want to change a situation, you do it without getting upset so that you don't throw yourself off balance.

WHERE DID WE GO WRONG?

We went off course when we forgot Pure Consciousness—our true Self—veiled one half of itself creating the *appearance* of duality. We, this creative consciousness that we are, did such a good job of creating the illusion of individuality and separateness that we believed it and forgot our real identity and our origin. Now lost and forgetful of the truth about our Source, we actually believe the illusion we see—a world separate and apart from ourselves with individual life forms functioning independently of one another. Influenced by the belief that we are alone and that we must succeed on our own, we continue to worry about our survival and take this game called life very seriously. As a result of this outlook, we have, to put it mildly, developed ways to survive that are contrary to our real Self and true nature.

LOSING TOUCH WITH REALITY

By identifying ourselves with our bodies and all things with their physical forms, we become separate from the Whole of Consciousness, taking on the qualities of the physical forms with which we identify. And since all physical form is *dense* matter, we become limited and unconscious as a result. At this stage, Pure Consciousness expressing itself as a human being is limited to the mere idea of itself, that of an entity operating independently of the Whole rather than an

149

expression of the Whole. Left with nothing more than this idea of ourselves, we are limited accordingly. In this state of ignorance, we live within the confines of our minds, never knowing who we are or where we came from.

Living within this illusion, we believe that our unconscious state and the limitations associated with it are quite normal. In fact, we accept our suffering as though it is a natural part of life, believing that our experiences are not enough to satisfy us. We begin to feel as though we're missing something and search aimlessly for more in hope of fulfilling our needs and desires. Losing touch with our natural state, we become weak and helpless at the effect of the experiences we encounter in life.

The irony of our condition is that our unwillingness to accept our experiences and our search for something more perpetuates the imbalance making it appear as though our suffering is the result of something quite real and justifiable. In view of our ignorance, we avoid and tune out those experiences associated with the cause of our unhappiness. We begin to look for pleasure and self-gratification in hope of finding relief without ever realizing that by avoiding our experiences, we cause our own suffering.

~

THE KINDS OF
EXPERIENCES YOU EXPERIENCE
HAVE NOTHING TO DO WITH YOUR FEELING
HEALTHY AND FULFILLED, BUT ACCEPTING
EACH AND EVERY EXPERIENCE DOES.

~

BALANCING MIND AND HEART

Having created the many aspects of itself in the physical world, this creative consciousness or God has but one purpose: to express the love it has for itself. This makes perfect sense and should come as no surprise since anything this expression of consciousness comes in contact with would have to be part of itself. However, because we, the expression of this consciousness, have forgotten our origin, we act as though we are strangers rather than expressing the love we inherently have for each other. Living in fear of one another and careful not to let our guard down, we stand ready to defend ourselves.

TAKING RESPONSIBILITY FOR OUR PLANET

Considering that we human beings are an extension of Pure Consciousness with the same creative potential, it would seem as though we have created one hell of a place. In fact, we have such a wild imagination that we have developed unusual character traits, which are deviations from our true nature, for example, hatred, anger, greed, fear, and a need for love. Personality traits like these distance us from who and what we really are, causing dissatisfaction, pain, and suffering.

The sad thing about life on this planet is that it continues the way it does because of our ignorance and our way of thinking. As a reflection of creative consciousness, we are responsible for the quality of our lives because the quality of our lives is directly related to how we use the creative power of our minds. Unaware of our own power and forgetful of our source and our purpose for being, our purpose now is to *remember*. The best way to do that comes from our experiences because our experiences mirror our thoughts. It's really quite simple—*stop resisting life's experiences and you can begin to learn from them.*

MAINTAINING THE BALANCE

Since we know this phenomenal world is a projection of One Mind founded on love, it's no wonder the life support that sustains this planet is love from the heart. It is through love and only love that we can expand the collective consciousness of all mankind, allowing us to reach our true potential and to unleash the unlimited creative power of the Mind. When man reaches this plateau, his creative ability will be extended, alleviating the lifelong struggle for peace and self-preservation.

Because all things are an expression of Pure Consciousness founded on love, the deciding factor over the quality of our lives and life on this planet as a whole is love. Therefore, everything on this planet can be balanced and in perfect harmony if people would express their real Self and true nature. And that inherent quality in everyone's nature is love—love from the heart.

~

THE
LIFE FORCE THAT
REJUVENATES ALL LIVING THINGS IS
LOVE.
IF YOU CHOOSE
NOT TO EXPRESS YOUR LOVE,
THEN YOU CHOOSE A LIFELESS EXISTENCE.

~

CHAPTER 23

THE REALITY OF EMPTINESS

*"Before heaven and earth had taken form
all was vague and amorphous.
Therefore it was called the Great Beginning.
The Great Beginning produced emptiness
and emptiness produced the universe."*

Huai-nan Tzu

The purpose of this chapter is to expand your consciousness beyond the realm of a physical reality. In order to accomplish this expansion, you must be willing to consider the possibility of something other than a world of physical objects. Occupying a body and seeing things in one form or another, your awareness is limited to objects placed in space and time. It is from this belief in a physical reality made up of objects and forms that you identify yourself with your body.

For example, when walking from one room to another, you don't try to walk through the wall. You walk around it or through an opening in the wall. You do so because past experience has shown you that you cannot walk through solid objects, and this becomes your reality. Now, with your consciousness limited to a physical reality of objects in space and time, you mistakenly identify yourself with your body.

Consider the possibility that in order to have an object with form and dimensions, there must be an opposite of that form, which in this case is space. The reason space is an essential part of the equation is that without the space around objects, you wouldn't be able to distinguish one thing from another. In fact, if there were no space, the objects themselves could not exist.

~

WITHOUT THE SPACE WE CALL NOTHING,
THERE WOULD BE NO WAY TO DISTINGUISH
WHAT WE CALL SOMETHING;
THEREFORE,
NOTHING MUST BE EQUIVALENT TO SOMETHING.

~

ABSOLUTE REALITY

Having realized that the relationship between physical objects and space is inseparable, you can take the next step by asking the question, "What is reality?" To get a clearer understanding of the answer to this question, you must think of matter or physical forms as *energy*. As a result of the interaction of particles in an electromagnetic field, there is a concentration of energy creating a *dense field*. This concentration of energy manifests in a particular area, causing that area to appear different from the space around it. In actuality, matter or the object present in any given space is fundamentally no different—other than in texture—from the space around it.

From this theory you can ascertain that matter is a concentration of energy that only "appears" to be something other than the space around it. This statement implies that the essence of what you call *something* is the same as what you call *nothing,* and the only difference is the way it appears to you.

Physics' quantum field theory substantiates this line of thinking. The quantum field theory tells us that matter consists of particles moving along waves, and when you observe matter, any attempt to measure a subatomic particle's position and velocity simultaneously cannot be done accurately. The reason is that when you try to determine the exact position of a particle, its momentum becomes uncertain. Conversely, when you try to determine a particle's exact momentum, its position is uncertain. This dilemma is so well known there's a name for it; it's called Heisenberg's uncertainty principle.

Even more interesting, when you try to identify matter such as a subatomic particle like an electron, it can appear one of two ways: as a particle or a wave. What you, the observer, see depends on your point of view or the way you look at it. This means you must always consider yourself as part of the equation, *or what you see,* because the observer, or the "participator," influences the outcome of the observed. At this point, you have to start thinking of reality in terms of the relativity of the observer to the observed. In fact, not only are they interdependent, they co-exist.

Taking this one step further, modern theoretical physics tells us that the presence of matter is a disturbance of the underlying field in a particular place. In quantum electrodynamics, this disturbance is thought to be a *concentration of energy manifest as photons or radiant particles of light* in a vibrating electromagnetic field. In other words, there is no difference between an object and the space around it.

Personally, I prefer not to try to identify physical reality through the quantum field theory of physics. Whether particles or waves, whether here or there, it's all the same. *It is.* And it can't be defined in any manner, way, shape, or form. Simply stated, Pure Consciousness or God, a creative conscious intelligence expressed in the form of energy, makes up our physical reality.

I cannot pass up the opportunity to point out the correlation between quantum field theory and one's own life experiences. As the uncertainty principal states, when we observe matter, what we see is relative to the observer, or to our point of view. By reflecting on this aspect of the uncertainty principle and applying it to our personal reality, we can gain insight into the relationship between our thoughts and our life experiences.

In other words your experience—what you see and what takes place in your life—is directly related to your point of view or how you look at things. And how you look at things correlates with your mind-thoughts, that is, with your ideas, your conclusions, and your beliefs. Consequently, *you* have a direct influence over what appears to be happening independent of you and out of your control. You and what you experience are interrelated; in fact, they co-exist. Without one you couldn't have the other. Take a moment and contemplate this.

THE IRREDUCIBLE REAL

The void or emptiness of space can no longer be thought of as nothing, but rather the *Irreducible Real*, and the forms within that space, the *Reducible Real*. In order to free yourself of the idea that binds you to a world of solid objects in space and time and to know the vastness of this Irreducible Real, you must experience the great void. You're probably wondering just how you're supposed to experience the vastness of space. This question arises out of your fixation on physical objects and your belief that only physical forms alone exist.

To be successful at this experiential process, you must be open to the possibility that you can experience space. To begin, give yourself plenty of time and situate yourself in a quiet place where you will not be disturbed. Look at any physical object, a chair, a table, or whatever you choose, and for a few minutes stay focused on it. Now shift your focus to the space around the object. Allow your awareness of this space to expand so that you are conscious of the space in the whole room and remain focused on the space for a few minutes. Now become aware of the space within the entire house or building you're in. With your eyes closed, expand still further and imagine the space between the buildings or houses, the trees and mountains, and finally the space between our planet and the other planets in our solar system. Stay out there for a few minutes and imagine all this space leading out to an open void.

UNIVERSAL CONSCIOUSNESS

As you experience this void and become conscious of its vastness, you expand your consciousness as well. This expansion takes place as you let go of the placement of solid objects set in space and time, leaving nothing but an open void. As you let go of your fixation on solid objects, your consciousness expands to fill the space it discovers. Letting go further, one's consciousness expands into the vastness of the great void, encompassing both the observer and the observed, merging with the undifferentiated Whole of Pure Consciousness.

If you let go of your body consciousness long enough, you would realize the common origin of all things and experience yourself as one with the Whole. However, by continuing to believe in a false identity and by limiting reality to your idea of it, you will never experience the vastness of your true Self. The choice is yours. You can hold on and remain where you are, or you can let go and explore the vastness of Universal Consciousness. So, what will it be?

~

IF YOU WOULD CONSIDER THE POSSIBILITY
THAT SOMETHING MORE EXISTS
OTHER THAN PHYSICAL FORMS,
YOU WOULD GIVE YOURSELF
THE OPPORTUNITY TO
EXPERIENCE IT.

~

CHAPTER 24

WHO WE ARE
WHERE WE CAME FROM
AND HOW TO GET THERE

*"The primary imagination
I hold to be the living power
and prime agent of all human perception,
and as a repetition in the finite mind
of the eternal act of creation in the infinite
I Am."*

Samuel Taylor Coleridge

We sentient beings and all physical forms on this planet are an expression of a conscious intelligence referred to as the Self or God. Using its creative power of Mind, this intelligence visualized itself in various physical forms, and from that mental image, it created those forms into physical existence.

And so it began: evolution, the expansion of consciousness from the lowest*, most undeveloped level on earth, that is, mineral, up to plant, animal, and finally to human being. Man, having evolved to the highest level, is now in the very image of his Creator,

---

*lowest: not pertaining to quality but to the expansion and refinement of consciousness with regard to the development of the nervous system affecting sense perception and the ability a conscious entity has to communicate and respond to the various stimuli in its environment.

with the same creative faculty of Mind. Hence, we humans have the ability to think and to creatively reflect those thoughts into existence, the same way this creative intelligence did when it created us.

The fact that all human beings have this creative ability means that what we are and the situations we find ourselves in are the result of our thoughts reflected into a physical reality—a reality stemming from our current level of consciousness that we are responsible for creating, in other words, an experience of ourselves brought about by what we think.

With this ability to think and create, we also have the capacity to realize and know ourselves (self-realization) as direct descendants of this creative intelligence, or God. However, because of our lack of knowledge and our unwillingness to submit to the calling of our higher Self, we remain descendants of the animal kingdom. Prior to realizing our divinity and experiencing the transformation from animal to a spiritual being, we function on a level of survival and fear, perpetuating the suffering that exists on this planet.

STRANGER IN A STRANGE LAND

In view of how the evolutionary process works, that is, consciousness expanding and elevating itself from one level to another, it's inevitable that prior to realizing ourselves as spiritual beings, we will find ourselves lost in what appears to be unknown territory. We can see the results of this dilemma in the suffering and uncertainty we experience in the course of our daily lives. All of this occurs and will continue to occur until each one of us realizes who and what we really are.

Of course, we can have realizations about something in a moment of clarity. But true and lasting freedom is not necessarily attained after a week of chanting, fasting, meditating, or attending lectures and seminars. There is simply no way to experience lasting freedom from insecurity, anger, uncertainty, fear, and self-inflicted suffering until we realize and accept our relationship with the Creative Source of our existence.

The relationship between ourselves and our Source can be compared to a parent/child relationship, the parent representing the Creative Source, or God, and the child representing man as the offspring. For example, if a child is having difficulty and doesn't realize that his parent can help, he will not think to ask for assistance. Even worse, if the child forgets who his parent is, it becomes impossible for the parent to reveal himself to his child, or for the child to recognize his father.

And so it is that we find ourselves lost without a helping hand to guide us on our journey through life, a condition that continues until we realize the truth about our existence. Upon realizing and acknowledging our inner being as the Divine Source, we transcend our individual idea of self (ego) and are reunited with our true Self or God, a process referred to as self-realization, spiritual rebirth, or enlightenment.

From that point on, providing we maintain this relationship and do not lose touch with our higher Self, we are guided intuitively where previously we were lost in the uncertainty of our unconscious state. Having attained this awareness, we can no longer avoid taking responsibility for our present condition. It becomes clear that the responsibility lies with each of us, not with some unknown God far off in heaven. The real question then isn't "If there is a God why doesn't he help us?" but rather, "Why don't we listen and help ourselves?"

LOST AND FORGOTTEN

If you're wondering how we got so incredibly lost that we forgot where we came from, I can assure you it wasn't easy, but we managed to do it just the same. Part of the problem stems from not being able to communicate with our Creator and Source on the physical plane. This lack of physical presence leads to a lack of faith and doubt that anything other than ourselves really exists. Of course, it's easy to say we have faith and that we really do believe. But faith built on fear and ignorance is blind faith, which is ill-founded and powerless, whereas faith built on truth, self-knowledge, and life principles is founded on certainty and strength. This lack of knowledge is the reason that we can pray to God for guidance and our prayers are not answered, and the answers to our questions are not heard.

For the most part, we humans are only aware of physical forms because we are tuned into the physical plane through our physical senses. With experiences limited to objects and things, we assume all that exists is what we can see and feel. It's this limited concept— our belief in a solid reality—that contributes to our ignorance about the Creative Source within, thus limiting our innate ability to intuitively know and communicate with it.

MAKING THE CONNECTION

If you're holding onto any doubt about the existence of this higher intelligence and its ability to communicate with you, look within yourself. Sit quietly for a moment and get in touch with your inner being. While sitting there learn to listen.

Be persistent, and don't be discouraged or lose faith if you ask a question and the answer doesn't come to you immediately. Remember this: don't expect more from your faith than you're willing to give and you'll never be disappointed. In other words, there is simply no sense in shooting for the moon before you have fuel for the rocket.

~

FAITH COMES
FROM KNOWLEDGE,
SO DON'T TRY TO TRANSFORM
THE WORLD BEFORE YOU EXPERIENCE
A TRANSFORMATION OF
YOUR OWN.

~

Take this moment to focus your attention inward. Be still. Become aware of the presence of your inner being. Learn to communicate with your inner self, that which knows all and never lies to you. Listen to what your inner being has to say, and know beyond a shadow of a doubt that you are not alone. You can find guidance within simply by asking. All you have to do is listen.

~

IF
YOU WANT
TO KNOW WHO YOU ARE
AND WHERE YOU CAME FROM,
YOU SHOULD BEGIN BY LOOKING IN
THE RIGHT PLACE—
WITHIN.

~

CHAPTER 25

CAN YOU KNOW YOUR CREATOR OR CAN THE PART KNOW THE WHOLE?

*"To know the truth
one must get rid of knowledge;
nothing is more powerful and creative
than emptiness."*

Lao Tse

For something to be known, there must be a knower, which implies a separation between the two. It's this space between the knower and the known, the observer and the observed, that limits one's knowledge of the subject. When you inquire about something, the very thought creates distance from the subject. You, the thinker, now separate from that which is in question and looking at it from a distance, can only know that part which is visible to you from your point of view. The reason for this is that you are always limited to your perspective, so all you can ever see or hope to know is an *aspect* of the subject inquired about.

Because absolute knowledge encompasses *all* that could ever be known about something, it can never be limited to anyone's idea or thought. The Absolute cannot be specified or qualified in any way; therefore, any idea about the Whole can only be an *aspect* of it—a possibility in an infinite number of possibilities. Since you are an aspect of the Whole, you, the observer, are a finite idea of the infinite.

THE CREATIVE SOURCE

The Whole is Pure and Absolute. It cannot be thought of because it is the creative *source* of all thoughts. It is the substratum or core with the potential to mirror the ideas of the observer into the physical plane as the observed. This planet is a reflection of that idea, and you, an individual soul, are the reflection of that idea with a body.

Think of it like this. You are out in space without a body but with the ability to think. Imagining the physical universe and yourself on the planet Earth, you open your eyes and find you are in the midst of your creation with a physical body as your center of operation. Your mind's idea of self—what you imagined—is now displayed around you, but forgetful of who you are and where you came from, you interact with all that you see as though it is something other than what you are.

~

THE
SOURCE
IS A SHINING
CORE OF PURE POTENTIAL.
LIKE A CLEAR MIRROR, IT REFLECTS
THE POINT OF VIEW OF THE OBSERVER
AND BECOMES THE OBSERVED.

~

THE DILEMMA

You are an integral part of the Whole; however, by inquiring about your source, your very thought separates you from it. Thus, the part can never know the Whole because *it is the Whole,* and at the mere thought of itself, it's reduced to a part with a limited view. Trying to answer the age-old question, "Can man know his Creator?" only adds to the confusion since the more you seek the absolute truth about yourself, the less likely you are to find it. What you will find is an unlimited number of aspects of the truth, none of which are the whole truth.

If you look at this question strictly from a physical point of view, it's easy to see how you could be misled into believing you are an individual operating independently of the Whole, when in truth *all that you see is within you, and you are an integral part of it all.* Ultimately, you are It, all of It. You just forgot!

~

THE

UNIVERSE

IS YOUR CREATION.

THIS PLANET IS YOUR TEMPORARY HOME.

YOUR PURPOSE FOR BEING HERE IS TO

REMEMBER IT.

~

PROCESS OF ELIMINATION

Ultimately, you can't know who you are, but you most certainly can know the personality traits that are not you, such as those qualities that don't meet the highest ideal. When you chip away at those traits that are self-destructive and alien to your true nature, what's left is who you really are, not some thought or idea of yourself. No ideas, conclusions, or beliefs separating you from who and what you really are. No distraction or uncertainty. No anxiety or fear. Just being. Being one with the Absolute.

~

SINCE
THE PART
CAN NEVER KNOW THE WHOLE,
YOU CAN NEVER REALLY KNOW WHO YOU ARE.
YOU CAN ONLY BE WHO YOU ARE,
SO
LET IT BE.

~

CHAPTER 26

Love
Communication
and the
Price We Pay to Be Right

"Man must evolve
for all human conflict
a method which rejects revenge,
aggression and retaliation.
The foundation of such a method is love."

Martin Luther King, Jr.

Until we give up the need to defend ourselves, we will find it impossible to truly communicate with one another. By continuing to hold onto our belief that we are right, we limit ourselves to that point of view alone. We are so preoccupied with defending our position that we can't see from anyone else's. In fact, we become so attached to our position, we get stuck on it.

When we live our lives this way, our point of view is all that we know and believe to be true. As a result, we are blinded by our own ignorance. The irony is that with such an obvious inability to communicate, rather than questioning our behavior, we continue our relentless pursuit to be right. Amazing, isn't it? We are willing to continue arguing and fighting with one another just to be right.

THE FIGHT TO BE RIGHT

Once you become aware of your position and how you are caught up in the survival tactics to defend it, the best thing you can do is to remain open-minded. You must be willing to accept another person's experience as being equally valid as your own, whether you see it that way or not. Remember this: it's just another view yet undiscovered by you.

The choice to remain open is yours. The next time someone has a contrary view that you find upsetting, try communicating without being defensive. Stop and ask yourself, "What am I fighting to hold onto and why?" If you're persistent you will be free from this compulsive need to defend yourself.

You're the loser when you have to be right. You get to keep your limited point of view and never experience anything more than that. Also, if you weren't so busy arguing, it might have occurred to you that people really don't care if you're right nor do they want to give up their point of view for yours. Once you realize this, you can stop wasting time trying to convince yourself and others that you are right and they are wrong. One more thing, no one has ever learned anything by being right. The reason is that, when you get to be right, that's all you get. Now, I ask you, is having to be right really worth it?

~

KEEP HOLDING ONTO YOUR POSITION,
AND ALL YOU WILL CREATE
IS A FUTILE CONDITION.

~

THE TRUTH LIES IN THE PARADOX

When one sets out to find the truth, at some point along the way he or she must pass through the door of paradox; however, this door remains closed to those who live in fear with a need to defend their ego. Since you have come this far, you must be ready to pass through this doorway. With an open mind, let us begin the journey.

Your inability to view things objectively stems from your ego's fear for its survival. The ego takes a position, and from that point of view, it continues to defend itself. Having taken up the ego's position, you see the world from its point of view, and it's not a pretty sight.

The reason the world is not seen as a pretty place from the ego's point of view is that the ego's concern is only with self-preservation and nothing more. This idea of oneself, or the ego, lives in fear, constantly on the alert to protect itself from attack. The ego's purpose in life is to survive at all cost because it knows no other way. In view of this, when looking through the ego's eyes, you see yourself as alone, separate, and apart from your Source and everyone else, a condition referred to in some religions as "the separation." This condition is the cause of your seeing things from a distance. And it is this distance that gives rise to opposites in your mind. Stuck on your position, you cannot see any view other than your own. What you see and experience from your point of view is what you believe to be true. Consequently, the truth lies in the paradox because each individual has a point of view which is the truth for that person. Therefore, to seek and find the truth is to find out that what is *isn't*, and what isn't *is*.

You are blinded by your own ignorance if you believe what you see and experience from your point of view is the absolute truth. The truth *is*. The ultimate truth about anything can never really be known because your knowing something is to know it merely from one point of view.

~

REMEMBER,
IN ORDER TO
ESTABLISH WHAT IS RIGHT,
YOU MUST ESTABLISH WHAT IS WRONG
WHICH MEANS THERE IS NO DIFFERENCE
BETWEEN RIGHT AND WRONG
EXCEPT THE WAY THESE
OPPOSITES LOOK TO YOU
WHICH IS RELATIVE
TO YOUR POINT
OF VIEW OF
THEM.

~

Ultimately, there are no opposites. No good or bad, no right or wrong. There is only what is, and then there's your interpretation of it. Of course, when you're at one end looking at the other, this may not appear to be true, but just the same, that's how it is whether you realize it or not.

If you understand this fundamental truth, you also understand why we have been in conflict with one another since the beginning of time. It's all because of our unwillingness to recognize another person's view as equal to our own. When will it end?

~

IT'S

NEITHER

GOOD NOR BAD

TO BE RIGHT OR WRONG,

SO DON'T GET STUCK BEING

HAPPY OR SAD, SINCE ALL THAT

PLEASURE AND PAIN ISN'T

WORTH PLAYING

THE GAME.

~

GETTING TO THE HEART OF IT

Love unites both the speaker and the one spoken to. It harmonizes and unites the subject with the object. Without love as the foundation for your communication, your ability to communicate is limited. By communicating, I don't mean telling someone what you think and having that person merely formulate their interpretation of it. I mean *getting through* and actually sharing your experience, and that kind of connection can only occur when the purpose of your communication is for the well-being of others.

Remember, in order to receive something, something must be sent, and you can't send anything as long as you are holding onto it. In other words, to communicate means to transmit or "send" something from one point to another. So, if what you're sending is for yourself and not solely for the benefit of another person, your communication can never be accurately received because your attachment to it keeps you from letting it go. It's that simple. The next time you're speaking with someone, if you feel as though that person didn't grasp what you're saying, look at your reasons for saying it.

∼

ONCE
YOU'RE OK
BEING WHO YOU ARE,
YOU'LL BE OK LETTING
OTHERS BE WHO THEY ARE.
UNTIL THAT TIME, YOU WILL CONTINUE
TO TRY AND CHANGE PEOPLE TO
YOUR WAY OF THINKING
BECAUSE OF YOUR
NEED TO DO
SO.

∼

TAKING A CHANCE ON LOVE
   Look for and see the best in people. Have compassion and understanding for those who would take

advantage of your openness and let your example show them the way. You see, love, communication, and your purpose for being here are interrelated. In fact, they are inseparable. When you realize that, I will have completed my communication with you.

Addendum

I want to thank you for giving me this opportunity to communicate with you, and I want you to know that I have the utmost respect for your courage to participate in work of this nature.

Love Always,

George Lavinia

P.S. May you get what you think and your thoughts always come from your heart.

If you would like information on lectures, seminars, tapes, additional books, and publications, or if you wish to participate in the volunteer program, you can call (212) 987-7587 or (800) 432-4680, e-mail earthfoundation@att.net, visit our website at www.earthfoundation.org, or write to:

The Earth Foundation
Post Office Box 462
New York, New York 10028

You may purchase additional copies of *What You Think Is What You Get* from The Earth Foundation by sending a check or money order with your mailing address to the address above in the amount of $12.95 plus $3.95 to cover shipping and handling. New York residents please add New York State sales tax.